THE QUICKENING

---

*"The world of the common man is about to
unravel, like never before. I seek the attention
of those who are strong and getting stronger. It
is only through the power of these 'individuals'
that the spirituality of the world will
survive the hurricanes of change.
There is little time."*

BY STUART WILDE

BOOKS

THE TAOS QUINTET:
Affirmations
The Force
Miracles
The Quickening
The Trick to Money Is Having Some

***

Infinite Self: 33 Steps to Reclaiming Your Inner Power
"Life Was Never Meant to Be a Struggle"
The Secrets of Life
Silent Power
Simply Wilde
Sixth Sense
Weight Loss for the Mind
Whispering Winds of Change

AUDIOCASSETTES

The Art of Meditation
Silent Power (audio book)
The Force (audio book)
Miracles (audio book)
Happiness Is Your Destiny
Intuition
Loving Relationships

Available at your local bookstore, or call **(800) 654-5126**

Please visit the Hay house Website at: **www.hayhouse.com** and
Stuart Wilde's Website at: **www.stuartwilde.com**

THE
QUICKENING

Stuart Wilde

Hay House, Inc.
Carlsbad, California • Sydney, Australia
Canada • Hong Kong • United Kingdom

Published and distributed in the United States by: Hay House, Inc., P.O. Box 5100, Carlsbad, CA 92018-5100 • (800) 654-5126 • (800) 650-5115 (fax) • www.hayhouse.com • **Published and distributed in Australia by:** Hay House Australia Pty Ltd, P.O. Box 515, Brighton-Le-Sands, NSW 2216 • phone: 1800 023 516 • e-mail: info@hayhouse.com.au • **Distributed in the United Kingdom by:** Airlift, 8 The Arena, Mollison Ave., Enfield, Middlesex, United Kingdom EN3 7NL • **Distributed in Canada by:** Raincoast, 9050 Shaughnessy St., Vancouver, B.C., Canada V6P 6E5

Book design by Jenny Richards
Cover Art by Ronsaville, Wood & Harlin

Library of Congress Cataloging-in-Publication Data

Wilde, Stuart,
        The Quickening / Stuart Wilde.
            p.   cm.
        Originally published: Taos, N.M., USA: White Dove International, 1988
        ISBN 1-56170-165-3 (tradepaper)
        1. Occultism I. Title.
        [BF1999.W5585 1995
        131—dc20   94-45490
                                                                         CIP

                            ISBN 1-56170-165-3

                        06 05 04 03   21 20 19 18

        First Published in 1983 by Nacson & Sons, Pty., Sydney, Australia

            18th printing by Hay House, Inc., January 2003

                Printed in the United States of America

To Robyne and Sebastien.
Please put the royalties in the
"sitting-on-the-beach" retirement fund.

Come to the cliff, he said.
They said, we are afraid.
Come to the cliff, he said.
They came.
He pushed them.
And they flew.

CONTENTS

1

HURTLING PAST HOCUS-POCUS

THE QUICKENING is a series of perceptions and Life Force (etheric) exercises that allow you to consolidate and accelerate your energy. It grants you the charisma and power to break out of the sluggish "collective" destiny of mankind, into a more glorious, heightened, individualized destiny of your own.

No doubt you have worked on yourself; in doing so, you have been exposed to every trick in the book. You have meditated, affirmed, visualized, wired two crystals up your nose, stuffed alfalfa sprouts in your ear, jogged around the block, and kissed swami on the toe. Here you find yourself, knowing that your inner reality is the only reality, and yet perhaps wondering why you do not have all your hopes and dreams at your fingertips.

You have reached what I call the "plateau of comfort." Things are okay, but you intuit that there is more. Now is the time for the

Quickening, the personalized, internal aggression that says, "I can achieve more. I have to become more; if not, I'll drift backwards."

As we look at the evolution of mankind, we see in its history the rise and fall of societies mirrored in the ebb and flow of greatness. Within those cycles, I believe, every so often the earth creates a cataclysm in which it cleanses itself of the imbalance of man's presence, and humanity is wiped out for the most part. In order for the human species to survive that cataclysm, there comes, near the "end-time," a teaching from the inner worlds—or the collective unconscious of man—that shows him how to step from his logical-thinking evolution into a higher spirit-man evolution, from which he can later progress into the safety of the etheric dimension—more of that later.

The Life Force (etheric) permeates all things. Once man develops the ability to be a part of that, meaning he can see the Life Force and understand it, it becomes possible for a few individuals to survive. This is not so much because they use their intuition to be in the right place at the right time, but more because they are able to step outside the collective destiny of man while still being a part of the physical.

This book talks of that inner teaching and of the Quickening that follows, and it shows you the doorway into the etheric world. If you become interested and want to know more, there is follow-up information at the back of the book.

Browsing in your local bookstore, you would not find many books on this subject, for the etheric is a hidden world. In order for us to penetrate that world, we've had to move to a different level of operation, and that took time.

At the beginning of this century, most esoteric, spiritual, and occult thought was dominated by the Theosophists, a society formed in the United States and later expanded to Britain and India. Five people (Madame Blavatsky, Annie Besant, C. W.

Leadbeater, H. Olcott, and A. P. Sinnett) wrote most of what we know to date of the etheric web, auras, magnetism, chakras, spiritualism, psychic perception, and reincarnation. These people took the ancient wisdom of the Hindus and translated them into a language Westerners could understand. Since then, little new has been added.

If, say, you read A. E. Powell's book *The Etheric Double*, you would see how he was influenced by the Big Five, and from his language you would understand that he wrote for his audience and his times, not ours. His book contains diagrams of *prana* bubbles heading back and forth through the chakra system. Yet once you read this, you will be little the wiser. The difficulty is that those writers wrote from concept, not necessarily from personal experience, and they were not ready, perhaps, to take concept into reality. Furthermore, their wisdom, which must have been very great given their point in history, was often couched in misleading terms. They talked to the reader as if he were as thick as two planks, which he probably was. Much of the real information was either hidden or not known. Practical ideas and methodology were omitted or wrapped in highfalutin terms and couched with a caveat to the reader not to get involved without a Master or an expert occultist—the name and address of whom was, of course, not offered.

Plus, if you come out of the modern-day, "get it together" philosophy, you are bound to ask all sorts of awkward questions such as, "How do I haul these *prana* bubbles down to the bank, Boo-ga-loo?" The answer is: You can't.

Then if you read the terms the writers used to describe energy, you can easily get lost in the "hocus-pocus." By the time you have waded through the etheric body, the astral body, the mental/causal body, the auric body, the psychic body, and two dozen other bits and bob, you are so confused you don't know if you're Arthur or Martha!

In my view, the Life, or etheric, Force is the one and only energy. All the terms used are just ways of expressing various aspects of the same etheric force. The etheric web that exudes from the individual is dense near to the body and less dense farther away. The less dense part is more susceptible to effects of thought-forms, for it takes on the energy of those thought-forms and contains within itself the striations they create in passing through. That part of the etheric I would call the aura.

Just as the aura is nothing more than a less dense, outer manifestation of the etheric, the mental and causal bodies are also etheric—or the patterns the mind and the emotions make in the etheric. The astral body is sometimes taken to mean a fantasy representation of one's physical body, flying through inner space. It can also mean the wraith that disengages from the physical body during the out-of-body experience. Again, that wraith is, for the most part, a fragment of the etheric web that you have disengaged from the physical. If you look at the various terms as meaning manifestations of the same energy, things clarify quickly, and you don't have to be swamped in the "hocus-pocus."

This book, *The Quickening*, serves those who like things fast and simple. It comes out being a somewhat brash philosophy, perhaps, but I feel that if a basic idea can't be put across in nine words or less, it can't be worth having. We are in the "hurry-up" brigade; we don't have time to plow through 60 pages of bubbles!

In addition, most of the old information is now obsolete and needs review. For example, most people believe that in order to protect themselves psychically, all they need to do is put a bubble of white light 'round their aura, with their mind. The reason they believe this is that the Theosophists put the idea out, and others, such as Dion Fortune in her book *Psychic Self-Defense*, parroted the concept.

In fact, if you understand the etheric, you will know that the white light bubble is not really of much use to you. Think of this—if you feel threatened enough to take time to attempt to defend yourself, that says a lot right there. In whatever situation you find yourself, if you do not feel that your energy is bigger than the situation, then it isn't. If it were, you would not be messing about protecting yourself. The action, in itself, contains an inherent affirmation of weakness.

A wimpy person with a shield is still a wimpy person. And because one's energy is not strong and consolidated, whatever shield one places around oneself with the mind rests on a brittle base and is easily penetrated. Imagine a midget confronting a 400-pound giant. The giant is holding an ax. The midget has his little bubble on. The giant steps forward and squashes him, bubble and all.

Now if that shield is all that you have going for you, fine, but your best strength comes from feeling centered and secure and knowing that the goodness of the Great Spirit is in your heart. It is impossible for you to defend yourself from every psychic intrusion projected at you. But if your inner essence is basically good, any psychic intrusion that may penetrate finds nothing on which to feed, and so, melts away.

Anyone who has learned to project the etheric mentally, in a concerted way, can get inside your aura. There is little you can do about it. If you think otherwise, you are flat-out wrong. Here's why: The root chakra, at the base of the spine, is always open, even if you are not sexually active. It is the storehouse of your Life Force. So your bubble is fine, but you've left the back door open. There is not much you can do about it.

Now I know some will disagree with me on this point. Recently I had a man stomp out of one of my seminars—in a huff because he presented courses and lectures on the "little bubble technique." He was not able to accept that his raison d'être was mostly baloney.

The point is, we have taken the sum total of esoteric knowledge for granted, operating through it as best we can. Yet, when we look for reasons as to why we have not empowered ourselves to the peak of perception, every item of our knowledge and methodology ought to be reviewed for its authenticity.

It always bothered me to hear about people with superhuman power—to hear of initiates who could walk through walls, levitate, bi-locate their bodies over vast distances, and read the minds of others. Yet where are all these bods today? What was their methodology? Surely, we are as powerful today as any society that has ever lived. Whatever was available to these supermen must be available to us.

I aimed to find out. I realized that the etheric was the place to start, for it is the gateway to the dead-zone between our world and the inner worlds. Once there, we can make our moves, providing we can get past the sheer terror that the etheric world seems to create for us. I want you to read this book, work on the techniques, penetrate the etheric, and prove it for yourself. Never mind reading a bunch of musty books: Let's declare ourselves in!

I studied for a number of years with a group of European occultists. Now if you refer to the occult in the USA, people think you mean black magic. This is not so in Europe, where there are occult brotherhoods, such as the Druids, that come out of goodness and a pure heart and have existed for a thousand years or more. These societies teach the rudiments of etheric perception, within the limits of their knowledge or of what they were prepared to impart. But I found it an excellent place to start.

My first realization was that most of the knowledge I had previously acquired was useless to me and had to be tossed out. As you begin the Quickening, keep an open mind as to the quality of the knowledge you think you know. It's true that the hardest people to teach are the experts, for coming from an energy of knowing it all, they exclude themselves from everything else. The Warrior-Sage admits to his ignorance and holds on to nothing. In doing so, he has access to everything.

Here is another example of the way misinformation becomes a part of our spiritual folk law. It is popular nowadays to visit practitioners who specialize in "aura balancing," who makes moves and passes over you to open your chakras. Question: How do you know for certain that an open chakra is better than a closed one? "It's obvious," you might reply. But is it? And does your chakra-balancing practitioner actually see the chakra, or is he working blind? Do you see it? Or are you just taking his word for it? How would you react if I told you that what you feel for the most part is the chakra rocking on its vertical axis? Would you know if that vertical rocking were beneficial? Would you know if what I say is accurate or not?

I'm not trying to drive you nuts. But it is important that we review our past efforts in the light of our knowledge as we realize that it has taken us only a certain way. We should now dump whatever is vague or obsolete. This is not judgment of other people's practices, just selection. Very possibly in the course of this book, I will stomp on your most cherished beliefs, and you may feel as if the whole Mongolian army has plowed through your garden. But my motivation is not to change what you are. I want nothing from you. It is honor enough that you would take time to read what I write. Rather, I hope to "rattle your cage" in a friendly way so that you look at what you do believe, in order to ascertain whether it serves you or not.

Many years ago when I began my own quest, I felt that I had to acquire something or other in order to become spiritual. I felt that if I gained knowledge or hung out with holy people, somehow that energy would transfer itself to me and I would get stronger. As I moved on and grew wiser, I discovered that spiritual growth has little to do with acquisition. More, it became a function of what I was able to discard.

The whole philosophy of the Quickening calls on you to

lighten your load and to set your spirit free. It asks that you step into the philosophy of the Warrior-Sage and embrace your individuality so totally that you have absolutely no reservations about who it is you are and about what your purpose is in life.

Before we go into the etheric information, let us review where the world finds itself today. Let us also look at the psychology of the Quickening, without which etheric perception and exercises become meaningless.

2

GROUP SOULS, ANIMAL MAN

IN LOOKING at how man has fared over the ages, we can extrapolate from past trends in his evolution and see what lies ahead. Then we can decide what is likely to occur in the future and whether or not that is what we want for ourselves as individuals.

In the beginning, the evolution of mankind came out of the waters. The first inhabitants of our planet were microorganisms that eventually developed into waterborne species and finally land mammals. These animals had—as they do today—a group spirituality or "group soul," meaning that all apes are a part of the "group soul" of ape. That "group soul" evolves as the apes evolve. As the apes developed over eons and eons, they became hardier and more complex. Eventually, a part of their "group soul" broke away to form our ancestor, ape-man. I believe that at some point the spirituality we now take for granted—that Higher

Self within us—breathed itself into ape-men, and they were transformed from highly evolved animals into "animal-men." These ape-men had an ego, an individualized evolution more complex than the original ape "group soul." They were, in fact, a lowly evolution of man. An individual ape-man was not far removed from his animal nature. But by virtue of the individualized divinity that rested within him, the Higher Self, he gradually moved away from his animal instincts and became a full-fledged human.

It was as if once the animals had developed to the point where the Higher Self could benefit from physical evolution, it became spiritually feasible for that Higher Self to descend into the physical and accept it as a learning experience. The cerebral function of the ape-man was enhanced by a connection to inner worlds via its Higher Self, and bit by bit its perspective changed. Animal-man developed rational thinking. Moreover, he developed a separateness or an individualized ego. He saw his needs and life as an individual and not as a part of the whole or the animal "group soul." Animal-man became, over time, "thinking-man"—by now completely removed from the evolution of animals. He could rationalize and grunt for the first time ever, "I'm starving, let's do lunch." There, evolution has rested, progressing through ever more complex forms of thinking-man to the present day.

The motivation of thinking-man is survival. His thought process is logical and mechanical. He is, in fact, "mechanical-man," to use Gurdjieff's term. He reacts compulsively to the dictates of his subconscious mind. It is almost impossible for him to create original thought, for his mind-set follows the logical patterns given to him. His sense of originality is sparse, and he is obsessed with his incantations to the gods of Survival. He runs insurance companies!

For mechanical-man, embalmed as he is in his personality/ego cult, reality is seen as being outside of himself. He feels little or no ability to control that reality. Life constantly does it to him. Thus, he searches for a place to lay the blame for his misery and, when he finds the culprit, he sues him. Sentenced as he is to perpetual insecurity, the disease of mechanical-man is reflected in the societies and institutions he creates, every aspect of which is designed to control and limit individual freedom in covert ways. The irony is that the people who design the institutions to control the masses are, in turn, controlled by the very same institutions because they believe in them and can't live without them. So, the jailer and the prisoner find themselves both in the slammer, both with no real freedom. In addition, mechanical-man will endorse his helplessness by creating gods outside of himself to whom he mumbles pitifully, begging for safety and comfort.

In the last hundred years, Western man rediscovered the mysticism of the Ancient Wisdoms and entered a new evolution whereby a few individuals began to accept the pantheistic concept that God is everything and that they are, in fact, God. With that came the perception that reality, though seeming to exist outside the individual, does in fact exist only on a subjective level, inside. That reality, because it belongs to the individual, is one's personal dream, and it can be manipulated for the highest good.

Once this concept was fully accepted, man entered into the realm of "spirit-man," one who has gone past mechanical-man and has rediscovered his eternal connectedness to all things. His mind no longer functions only for his pleasure and as a record-keeper, but can now be used to do the work of pulling to him the reality he seeks. Thus, spirit-man is able to cut short a long and arduous journey through anguish and confusion by directing his consciousness with the psychic tension of his will. He quickens his life by focusing on whatever goals he pleases. He is able to maneuver his destiny somewhat; able to exist with one foot in the physical, the other in a higher evolution.

So we find ourselves today, with much of humanity still in thinking-man mode and an ever-increasing number expanding their awareness into spirit-man mode. It is the spirit-mode people who will step across the boundaries of evolution to experiences considered impossible by mechanical-man, and it is spirit-man who will eventually save the world. He will do this not in the sense that mechanical-man would like, whereby everything is cozy, safe, and guaranteed, but in the spiritual sense, whereby spirit-man will see within the chaos a thread and will follow it. It is spirit-man's alignment to the Life Force, his selflessness, his ability to follow the path guided by his Higher Consciousness, that allows for the survival of mankind. This is partly because spirit-man can step outside the general evolution and view the world in an objective way, and partly because it is through the concepts of the spirit-mode that he eventually enters the etheric dimension—that heightened quasi-physical dimension of pure Life Force that does not necessarily follow logical reasoning.

To enter the spirit-mode takes courage. You have to dedicate your life to yourself. This is not an egocentric view—more an act of prayer unto yourself. It does not make you more important than the world you live in; you just *become* the world you live in. It forces you to feel settled when there is no logical reason to be so. It calls you to ride as companion to uncertainty, caring little for that which concerns mechanical-man. It demands that you walk alone and be your own judge. You become your own advisor and teacher because there is no one who knows more about your life than you do. It allows you to evaluate mass consciousness in the light of your needs so that you are not rushed along mindlessly by the fads of the day.

The Harmonic Convergence was a good example of how you can sucker most people into almost anything if your story is good enough. For the benefit of those of you who were on the moon that week and didn't hear about the convergence, this is what happened: A man named Jose Arguelles came up with the theory that in mid-August, 1987, a whole bunch of planets would converge and that this planetary convergence coincided with the end of the Mayan calendar.

This portentous event was supposed to herald the coming of a new age—providing that at least 20,000 people gathered to celebrate the day. If the 20,000 had not gathered, no doubt some grizzly fate would have befallen us here on earth. Well, the whole spiritual New Age movement got involved, and in the end, millions of people observed some kind of spiritual practice on Convergence Day, which no doubt saved our skin, destiny-wise.

At our office in Taos, New Mexico, we held a special early-morning meditation, fasted, and did good things. It was a very quiet day. The phone hardly rang at all; most of our customers were up a mountain somewhere. Around four in the afternoon, bored out of our brains, we decided to close up shop and do our Harmonics at the pub.

The discussion turned naturally to the Convergence. It seemed that none of us really knew anything about it, nor had we ever met any Mayans, nor did we know anyone who knew any Mayans. We weren't even sure where the Mayans lived, although an impromptu poll held among the clients at the pub decided that the Mayans lived in Central America, probably in Mexico.

Then, we realized that, if we looked at it truthfully, none of us really cared whether the Mayans had a calendar or not. We felt sorry that their calendar had fizzled out, but there was not much we could do about it. Someone suggested an international Red Cross airlift of surplus calendars, and I offered one that I had gotten from Ricky's Auto Parts that I didn't use that much. It was none too spiritual—it had a nude on the front, holding a wrench. But I thought perhaps that the Mayans could muddle along with it until something better came along. We concluded the discussion wondering what Mayan kids who came into the world after the Convergence would do. How would they know when they were born or when to expect birthday presents?

The upshot of all this convergence stuff was that we had a good laugh, for we learned how easily we had been suckered into the thing. Isn't it strange that no one asked for a real explanation? Everyone seemed happy to follow along with the theories of a complete unknown, like Arguelles, regardless of whether it made sense or not. The fact that there is a *Quickening* going on is obvious. But to put it down to a hard-to-find Mexican tribe that has run out of dates is bananas. We resolved to stay more awake in the future.

It seems to me that the first animals that developed on the planet, out of the microbe soup, must have been assisted by energies in an inner, higher evolution. Perhaps it was some deva or spirit authority, or what we would call, in our simplistic way, angels. These overseeing bodies carried the animal evolution through the critical period from microbe to ape and then on to where the ape was accepted by the divinity of the Higher Self and became ape-man. When you look at, say, the complexities of the ape's digestive system, it seems to me impossible that such a system could have developed as a biological accident from the original microbe soup.

I know the popular idea is that if you put a hundred monkeys on typewriters banging away at random for a million years, in the end you will have a Shakespearean play. I just don't buy into that. If you look at the biological makeup of an animal's body, it has order and vast complexity. To say that this order and complexity came about at random, regardless of how many years were involved, is pretty loony. Chaos does not evolve into order unless there is something acting on that chaos to direct it into a system.

Here is one explanation to mull over. What if some Higher Power worked on a form of genetic engineering and through trial and error molded the original microbe soup into the various

species we find on earth? The insects and fish and less complicated animals being, for the most part, practice shots, until finally the Higher Power got it right, creating the ape and the chim-
panzee. And then the Power realized that it was only one chro-
mosome away from a human. Bingo—human evolution!

What if that same Higher Power did not realize at the start
that human evolution was possible? As it began working on the
microbe soup, it could see that there were myriad possibilities in
the makeup of the soup. But what if that Power had to develop its
own perception and knowledge for a few billion years before it
could see that from the soup into the living things of the waters,
and through the eventual land-based life, there was the exciting
possibility of an animal that thought for itself.

It is possible also that the Higher Power that started working
on the microbe soup was not the same Power that eventually got
the DNA right and created man. It is possible that once evolution
reached the critical cusp of moving from animal to ape-man, and
the Higher Selves that would eventually enter the physical plane
got ready to make their first moves, that perhaps a very Great
Power had to oversee this in order for it all to be in balance. To
say that God did it is to say, basically, "I haven't a clue." But it
must have been more complicated than God knocking it out
Monday during the ball game.

We can see that the female of the human species holds the
natural balance of our planet. Her spirituality is closer to the God-
Force than is the male's. His energy is to the side of, or oblique
to, the naturalness of things. Now, we could have had a population of hermaphrodites, part female, part male, who mated with
themselves. But obviously having two slightly different DNA
molecules made human evolution stronger and more durable. The
male acts as friction or acidity to the natural spirituality of the
female. In turn, he provided, in the early days, anyway, the brute
force and protection she needed in her reproductive time, when

she was the least mobile and the most vulnerable.

Isn't it interesting that the sex urge is in just the right balance? Forceful enough to ensure the propagation of the species—evidenced by the fact that folk seem to take to the activity with great gusto—yet not so strong as to wreck the joint. The male had to be persuaded to act as the provider/defender, and the female had to find the sex act satisfying, otherwise she would not have conceived and brought to term the future population.

If the sex urge had been too aggressive in the male, the early females would have shunned his company, through fear. If it had been painful, folks would have taken up knitting. If it were weaker, the human race would not have had the population base in the critical early days, and we would not have survived. How was this fine balance achieved? Who figured out how much testosterone and sperm the male needed or how the female egg would flow, or what level of urge would ensure the planet's survival and yet not have it careening out of control? Again, is it a biological accident, or did someone, somewhere, experiment until they got it right, or what?

As we look at these baffling questions, it seems to me a fair conclusion that something directed the operation, and that something had a vested interest in getting the program right. The question is: What was its motivation? Who did it?

3

TURBO-THOUGHT

IF YOU have read my book *Affirmations*, you will recall that I described journeys I have taken up the tunnel of light into the spirit world. These journeys were performed in trance. I believe the tunnel to be the same as that described by people who have had near-death experiences. It is the etheric link between our seemingly outer physical world and the inner worlds of spiritual evolution. On the other end of the tunnel, the light of the God-Force shines, unrestrained by the limitations of the human brain, which acts as an inhibitor for humans, keeping them focused in the physical. That light is pure energy. We perceive it as unconditional love.

One of the things we know about that energy is that is seems to have intelligence, but it does not seem to have volition. Meaning, it does not seem to have a mind or desire of its own. Note that I use the word *seem*. I cannot categorically state that its lack of volition is a fact. It may have volition, but one that is beyond our comprehension. Perhaps its desire or volition is hidden from our view. Perhaps the cycle that the God-Force is in is so infinitely long in human terms, that in viewing the light we see it between breaths or thoughts. Imagine a single electromagnetic oscillation that takes a million years to complete. There would be a point of balance at the halfway stage when the electromagnetic force would look static. Perhaps the God-Force is between throbs—the next one not due for a half-million years. I know that might sound nutty, but think of those cacti that flower every 12 years, for a day or two. You could be forgiven for thinking that they did not bloom at all.

The inner light that manifests as the etheric in our plane is passive and egoless. It shines and can be used, but it does not tell one what to have for breakfast. It is an emanation of the God-Force expressed in a weaker form. Could it be that the Life Force or God-Force that we experience is in fact the tension between the two polarities found in the human cell? Is it that and more, or just that? Could it be that the power in the cell is in fact the inner light? I think it likely.

Moving on, we see that it is unlikely that the Life Force brought about the evolution of humans on this planet, the Force not having a volition in human terms. So whatever motivation prompted man's evolution, it was most likely not a motivation of the God-Force but of some other entity or group that knew how to direct the God-Force. Could it be that human evolution on earth is so insignificant and is so far removed from where God concentrates its energy that some lesser entity took on the project? We know that if a person learns to identify with the etheric, he or she can soon be taught to project it, creating thought-forms that are laced with the etheric and are powered by concentration and the force of will. These specially formulated thought-forms can be seen and felt by others. They contain more intensity than normal thought, and their trajectory is more clearly defined.

How do we know this to be true? Over the years, I have developed a system for taking a concentrated thought-form molecule of the ego/identity—a millionth part, say—wrapping it with etheric Life Force taken from the body, accentuating it with concentration and force of will, and firing it like a dart. I call it "turbo-thought." I have taught this technique to about 1,700 people around the world. We know from our experiments that the average, dedicated individual can be taught these methods over a period of a few days. At the end of my teachings, I ask people to go out into the town and find a barking dog. If they can hold that dog with their mind for 30 seconds and force it to stop barking, I know that the individual has the technique down pat.

Because these special turbo-thoughts can be seen, a part of their intrinsic makeup must have mass. Although the thought-form is invisible to the naked eye, one can see the striations or lines it makes as it flies from the individual's mind through the etheric web around the body, in the same way a nuclear physicist never sees subatomic particles but can watch the trajectory that those particles make when they collide. From that, he learns how they behave.

We know that these special turbo-thoughts can be felt by humans and animals alike, and we know their power to be awesome. When fired correctly, they can force a person to turn around, blink, or make some unusual move. In Europe, I hung out with a group who had mastered the turbo-thought technique. They never actually taught me the techniques, but they claimed that such thought, properly directed, could stop a human heart. Years later I realized this was true.

Recently, I tried an experiment with an occultist friend of mine. The idea was for me to project an enhanced turbo-thought, not one that would stop his heart, but one designed to momentarily arrest his respiratory system. Tricky stuff and very dangerous, so forgive me if I skip the methodology on this one. Anyway, 15 minutes into the experiment, the subject went into a respiratory crisis which, in less than 30 seconds, began to develop into mild asphyxia. I pulled back once I realized the subject was approaching the danger zone. He recovered immediately.

The experiment proved to me that a thought, if strong enough, could interfere with the life-sustaining functions of the body. It is interesting to ponder the extent of the influence that the mind can exert. When I lived in Ghana, I heard stories of JuJu shamans being able to kill a person with their magic. The stories were fairly common, and the locals treated the JuJu with great respect. It was said that the JuJu could not kill a white man, because he did not believe in it. This was not correct, and there were several stories of Europeans dying in mysterious circumstances at the hands of the JuJu. One theory to explain the JuJu's power was that once the victim knew that he had been hexed by the shaman, the victim then basically killed himself with fright. This may have been so, but what of those cases where the victim was not aware of the JuJu's hex? The old black magic traditions in Europe are replete with tales of people being bumped off by the local witch.

The fact is that when the mind is powerfully directed, it can exert much more influence than is generally assumed. We know that it can move a physical object, provided the object is light. Now as humans we develop out of a skimpy amount of Life Force. But what if the entity or entities that directed our evolution were, say, a million times more powerful than us? Would it not be possible for them to mold their own version of turbo-thought onto the microbe soup and move the etheric in whatever direction suited their ends? From what we know of our abilities and our methodology, which probably looks hokey from the inner worlds, it would seem a very real possibility that something somewhere was able to direct or at least guide things here on earth.

That something would have to be incredibly powerful. We would consider it to be God. But perhaps, on the infinite scale of things, it is in fact pretty wimpy, and beyond it are bigger and even more powerful energies that it, too, considers, God. Perhaps

"God" is just a way of saying that there is an energy oscillation up ahead that is bigger than I am!

I am not much into the idea that spacêmen set up the original evolution here on earth. I am sure that in many places in the universe there must be other forms of life, but because of the distances involved, their influence has been nonexistent or minimal at the most.

There is one other theory that offers food for thought. Close to the physical plane, in the etheric world, there are quasi-physical beings. They live in a dimension of the etheric that is very close to our reality. Their energy is repulsive to us, for they are animal, yet they possess the grosser human emotions. Some say that the Yeti and Big Foot are examples of these evolutions. These energies are less evolved than humans, but are close to us in form and motivation. One theory suggests that these beings were evolving in a dimension parallel to the physical and that at some stage they walked across the threshold, thus populating the earth. The theory holds that humans evolved in an upward direction from these beings and that the ape and the chimp are in fact a part of the same evolution, but that they evolved downwards from man, rather than the other way around.

Where is all this ape-man stuff leading us? The drift goes like this: If you accept that evolution on this plane is too complicated to have happened without direction, then you may also accept that our evolution here is still complicated and that perhaps, in the inner worlds, there is a Force or entity or group of some kind that knows where we are all going. Perhaps that Force is directing us or helping us to some conclusion. Perhaps that Force is only now allowing us to penetrate its world somewhat so that we can learn. Perhaps we have just evolved to the point where we are able to learn.

As we become more metaphysically sophisticated, many of the old questions can no longer be covered over. The idea that

Jesus' dad is doing it works fine for hundreds of millions of people. It allows them to go back to the TV. But there are also many millions who want to know more, who consider the simplistic tribal ideas fine, but who know there is a reality beyond normal perception. They aim to find out, for they consider it vital.

The problems of the world seem insurmountable. Three possibilities offer themselves. The first is that we don't fix the problems and the world descends into chaos, that population wilts, and the survivors return to the caveman stage. The second is that the world descends into chaos, but within that chaos a small group of metaphysically sophisticated people with learning from the inner worlds survives. The third is that somehow the world learns to go beyond its problems and survives more or less as we know it today. But don't bet the farm on that! I know it is popular to think that technology will bail us out, yet when you look at our technological progress you see only little Japanese digital boxes that open cans while whistling Dixie. You don't see spiritual solutions. All the computers in the world won't stop the stock market from crashing, and, ironically, for the most part, they won't even stop the owners of those computers from losing their shorts. The chance that we can fix things is now so remote that it is not really a serious consideration. But we live in hope.

Perhaps the *Quickening* we feel at this time is the end rush of a wind that will carry man to his rendezvous with destiny. Certainly, we know that time is of the essence and that the great divide between the metaphysical haves and the metaphysical have nots will be accentuated over the next decade. You either jump from the wimpy-dimpy, wet-lick-in-the-ear philosophies that whine their "save me, love me, tell me I'm okay" dirges to Warrior-Sage, or you don't. In the end, no one cares except you—and that is the way it should be.

4

REALITY, CATACLYSMS, SPOON-FED SOCIETIES

WHATEVER THE theory as to how we got our start, there was a dramatic point when evolution went from animal to animal-man. A major change took place. Man was suddenly able to differentiate between what was outside of himself—external to his reality—and what was not. A separation took place. A dog, say, cannot intellectualize or differentiate between what is a part of itself and what is not. It does not know that the tree exists outside of itself, for everything to a dog is inner, or subjective. Animal-man, possessing for the first time an individualized Higher Self, went through "the fall" and experienced through his intellectual faculty a separateness. He could see reality outside of himself, and he thought that there was a difference between him and other things. It is only now as we enter the age of spirit-man that we complete the fall and get back to an internalized reality, feeling, through our spiritual alignment, a part of all things.

The question posed throughout the ages is: Is the external reality the true reality, or is our internal reality the true reality? The fact is, both are real. The mechanical thinking-man sees the tree outside of himself, and he will logically conclude that there is a reality outside of himself. The spirit-man, coming out of feelings rather than logic, will say, "I feel that I am a part of all things; the tree feels as if it is inside of me, for when I sit still, I can feel its sap rising within my own body." Therefore, reality must also be an inner experience.

In the end, the argument is irrelevant, for the truth is that none of us experiences true reality. When looking at a red fire engine, the brain does not actually see the color red. What it accepts is the wave oscillation of light reflected off the fire truck, and that light contains all colors except red; the oscillation we call red never reaches the brain. In other words, it is the absence of red that makes the fire truck appear red. So, as you look at reality, what you are looking at is everything other than what is there. By looking at all light and eliminating what is not there, you see and comprehend what is there; that is, one red fire truck.

What happens to the light reflecting off the fire truck that you do see? In fact, the brain has no ability to see that colored light either. The light image hits the eye upside down and creates an oscillation of the optic nerve, and it is that oscillation that is carried to the brain, not the color. The oscillation contains none of the original light or color. It is just a representation or wave length of that light/color. Once it impacts the brain cells, there is a mechanism there that turns the image up the right way and reads the oscillation. The brain knows how to translate that into a color code it understands, but the brain has never seen true reality. The point is, what you believe to be reality or truth is, in fact, the absence of reality, upside down, translated by your brain from a wavelength into what seems to be the undeniable truth. "That fire truck is red; I'll stake my life on it." Are you sure?

Thus, for people to argue about the nature of reality and truth is pointless, an intellectual masturbation of unparalleled uselessness. Reality is subjective, personal to you. There are as many realities and truths as there are people to perceive those truths. A million people may agree that taking another's possessions without his permission is stealing and morally wrong, but that is just their opinion. As you step into spirit-man mode, you learn not to adhere to absolutes, not to define too closely what is and what is not. Logic melts in the light of infinity and in the changing dimensions of consciousness. Although stealing is morally wrong to us, there may be a dimension wherein taking other people's property is not stealing, where it is not wrong for reasons we cannot understand.

If you leave thinking-man to his logic, the destiny of the world as we know it demands that it will end. Its resources are finite, the population is expanding, and pollution is almost unstoppable given the opinions of the masses who say jobs, factories, and Styrofoam cups are more vital than forests and ozone layers.

The popular theory is that as the world wheezes to a halt, the imbalance created in nature sets up adverse electromagnetic forces that eventually tip the poles, and the whole world, in a matter of 20 minutes, experiences a cataclysm of unimaginable proportions. The effect of this sudden pole shift, whereby the north-south axis becomes the new equator, would create tidal waves many miles high and winds of several thousand miles per hour. It is postulated that the dust created by this event would hang in the air 300 years or more. Some say that the story of the Garden of Eden is set just after the last cataclysm and that this is why the Garden was so rich and verdant.

Whether all this is true or not is irrelevant to spirit-man, for survival is not his motivation. That is why he *will* survive. But it is not the focus of his attention. Does the night-blooming flower spend the night counting the hours till dawn? The concern with the cataclysm is a thinking-man's reaction. The fact that the world as we know it is about to fall apart is obvious. Just when that denouement will take place needs to be decided by the people. The vote is cast by their lack of concern, the lack of higher consciousness, and the inability of the Mickey Mouse leaders to see beyond the next election.

Now you may say, "That's a shame, we ought to do something about it." You are right, but what can we do? The people choose Mickey Mouse leaders because they want spoon-fed societies with policies that appeal to thinking-man's need for security, not nations built on a metaphysical balance or correctness, which would appeal only to a minority—those in spirit-man mode.

If America voted in, say, a powerful President who came from a spirit-man, metaphysical balance there would be rioting in the streets the day after the inauguration. The security fears of the masses would be so rattled that mayhem would ensue. The new President would not be concerned with coddling the people in phony prosperity; he or she would center on a metaphysical reality and would pull the rug out from under the guarantee.

In the same way, the weak fall by the wayside in the forest, so does a metaphysically strong society have to contain the possibility of individuals' collapse and destruction in order to motivate the masses. That is why America was such a powerful society in the early days of the pioneers. If, while walking across America with your wagon you broke a leg and fell sick, you probably died. Thus, the pioneers were careful to stay in balance, for the consequences were awesome if they did not.

In our modern society, if you fall, someone, somewhere, will catch you. In the subconscious mind of the people, the propensity to stay in balance is less. The society becomes weak and self-indulgent and turns to all manner of stimulation to titillate itself, rather than live in the natural excitement of never knowing if anyone will make it through the day or not.

Does this mean that our mythical new president would allow people to die in the street? Probably not, for that is just too real, too harrowing. But he or she would allow the possibility of imminent disaster to motivate the people into looking after themselves. Isn't it true that your most industrious and creative moments have almost always been at times when you faced ruin or financial collapse? Your mind got the message; you hurtled into the marketplace and did some crafty things to fix the problem.

The consciousness of thinking-man is not elevated enough for him to accept total responsibility for himself. Self-reliance, devoid of survival fears, is not natural to him, for he lives in an ego that is obsessed with itself and its survival.

History repeatedly shows us civilizations that collapsed once they became too self-indulgent. What keeps a nation strong is a perpetual thought-form from the hearts of the people saying, "We are self-reliant, we are strong, we will work as hard as necessary to sustain our independence and individuality." Once that feeling is destroyed, then it is only a matter of time before the society collapses. With 38 million Americans living on government handouts, that thought-form melted sometime ago. But things will change.

5

THE ETERNAL STANCE
OF THE WARRIOR-SAGE

ONCE YOU understand the difference between thinking-man and spirit-man, you have only to look at the motivations you hold and determine from which mode they come. Are you part of the self-indulgent habits of thinking-man, or are you in the expansive but less secure lifestyle of spirit-man? It is simple to align with spirit-man intellectually, but less simple to do so emotionally, for you must step into a divine, infinite reality that quickens but also leads you into the unknown.

The concerns of spirit-man are his levels of energy and the inner impact he creates for himself, not his staying alive. Spirit-man sees himself as eternal and prays only that his path may be well trod, with honor. He does not seek end results and is detached from concerns about life and death, political change, or social structure. Spirit-man rests within himself and is busy manipulating his own life, not the lives of others.

The world peace movement is an area where many spiritually conscious groups are maneuvering to change the way people think. That is very laudable. Yet the movement is firmly rooted in thinking-man's survival mode. It creates within man a yearning for something he does not have. It is like people who spend all their life miserably grasping at the straw of security only to discover that there is none and that security is irrelevant to the Higher Self.

I was flying recently from Washington, D.C., to Texas and picked up an in-flight magazine. The main article was a report from one of those government bodies that counts things. Well, it wasn't actually that body. The report came from a committee appointed to ensure that the department that did the counting, counted the stuff correctly. It seems that there are five million people at war in the world today, and the report "tut-tutted" and moaned about the various conflicts among the people of our planet.

It occurred to me as I read the article that if we have five million people at war, then with a planet of five billion souls, we have a total of four billion nine hundred and ninety-five million people who are not at war. This is all in all a fairly decent result when one considers our diverse cultures, the shortage of certain resources, and the level of discomfort that many sustain. Then the article went on to review the world refugee problem. It turns out that we have 15 million refugees in the world. My first thought was: How do the government officials in D.C. get the refugees to stand still while they count them? By their very nature, refugees wander about a lot. Aside from that thought, we can see that there are four billion nine hundred and eighty-five million folk who aren't refugees. Tonight they will all go home somewhere. Even if home is just a mud hut under a palm, it's still home.

In mechanical-man mode, you can easily get sucked into mass hysteria. In spirit-man mode, you would see war as undesirable, but since most of the world is uncomfortable and frustrated with itself, war follows naturally. It is a part of people's growth. You would know that for the masses there are precious few opportunities for metaphysical experiences. Childbirth, orgasm, and war are three. It is through these that the masses feel for a brief moment a connectedness to all things. Why would you take that away from them?

To sustain the *Quickening* within, one has to begin to dry-clean one's feelings from emotional attachments and needs. This involves giving up those areas of opinion that no longer serve. Each place where one is emotionally attached creates a line, like a grappling hook, that binds one to the consciousness of tick-tock. To go beyond, one has to disengage. Otherwise, the weight of emotional concerns do not allow one to rise above the "plateau of comfort" into a consciousness that develops critical mass.

The power needed to accelerate you past your current state is great indeed, and the more stripped of emotion you are, the less opinions you hold, the less rigidity you create, then the more your ability to break out of the gravitational grip of the "collective" consciousness is enhanced by the lightness of your load. You can't be different and hold the same feelings as the mass of people.

To establish that difference, you need to create an emotional barrier between yourself and the world. It is a psychic demarcation zone through which no emotion will pass. It becomes the buffer between you and life's circumstances.

This buffer is developed in several ways. First you pull away from the desires and attachments that you have about your own life. You voice no opinion. You just accept reality as you find it, internalize it, and own it even if you do not like it. This does not mean you cannot change things if you wish; it just means that the way things are is the way they are, and you have to be able to accept that. Any negative yearning that you have about your life serves only as an affirmation of weakness and locks you in.

Nowadays, people insist that everything be perfect, safe, comfortable, and convenient; and so often life is not any of these. The Warrior-Sage accepts discomfort and pain and rides on, regardless. His life is not regulated by having to have this or that. He does not demand that conditions be perfect, or even to his liking. He learns to stay centered whatever the circumstances. By not reacting to your surroundings and by ignoring the emotional gyrations of others, you empower yourself from within.

Anytime one reacts to events and conditions, one flips back into thinking-man weakness. Reaction is an affirmation that, first, one doesn't control events and, second, one considers reality to be that which is outside of oneself. By accepting and internalizing reality, one affirms that one's life is one's own creation, that you and only you control it.

The buffer zone one creates around oneself contains at its center a powerful affirmation that says:

> *I accept myself.*
> *I am not perfect.*
> *I have aspirations to become*
> *more so, but I accept myself.*
> *Therefore, I can accept the life*
> *I am living for I have created it.*
> *Today is my day; I am what*
> *I am within whatever I find,*
> *and nothing can push me*
> *off that balance.*

The mind of thinking-man contains myriad opinions as to what should be. Each opinion is an affirmation of thinking-man's pathetic state of weakness. It is only an opinion that says that one's body should be strong and healthy. It is only an opinion that says that one should live a long life. What if you don't? Are you going to negate the time you have spent on earth? Who says one has to be rich and wear fine clothes and be treated in a special way? Who says you have to sleep so many hours and eat so many meals? Where is it cast in stone that you have to be dry and warm and safe? What if you find yourself in a place that is freezing, wet, and dangerous? Do you moan your way into missing the experience, or do you open to acceptance from strength?

Mechanical-man trots through his miserable little rhythms of life and misses it for the most part. This is why most of the people you meet are as dull as dishwater. They have optioned themselves out of life and have nothing to offer. They may live to be 99, but their experiences are of little worth. They still don't accept themselves, and they are still uncomfortable. It is better to live as a Warrior-Sage for 30 years and to accept the experience of life than it is to cast oneself into the living hell of the stereotype.

Once that acceptance of self is complete, the gateway to the other worlds opens, and not before. One has to operate from strength. By accepting life as it comes, with all its anguish, frustration, and pain, one affirms one's eternal stance within reality. You say, "I am what I am, and what I am is centered and confident, regardless of what is happening; I am that Higher Self within which I am granted honor and nobility; everything else is irrelevant."

The weak never accept where they find themselves. They always want to change things, even when changing things is not worth the effort. Their inner discomfort demands a constant restlessness. Once the Quickening is a part of life, you will not care whether things change or not, and you will not feel the need to change things other than yourself, for you will develop a comfortable, stable acceptance of self. You will be happy to let things be, and you will allow others to do the campaigning. They'll need it; you won't.

6

INVISIBILITY

WHEN YOU don't have to change things, you become free, for
you move through the etheric of the world without disturbing it. In one way, it makes you invisible. Imagine your life
in these terms: You are a warrior. You have to scale the walls of
an enemy castle at night without disturbing anyone. On the battlements roosts a flock of geese. The slightest error or sound, the
minutest disturbance—a pebble tumbling onto the rocks below, a
cough—and you are dead. How will you do it?

You would have to be very confident of your abilities and
very aware of your surroundings. You would take time to scope
out the castle in minute detail. You would adapt to the circumstances by wearing dark clothes. You would check and double-
check all the resources available to you—your equipment, the
nooks and crannies, the phase of the moon, cloud density, any
covering noise that would assist you, such as, say, a thunder-
storm. And you would make sure before you set out that your tim-

ing was right to ensure that your assault was not made on a night they doubled the guard. But most of all, you would think in terms of moving in silently and moving out again, touching nothing, disturbing nothing. That is the energy of the Warrior-Sage.

Try this etheric exercise: Go to a crowded place, such as a shopping mall on a Saturday. Center your concentration completely inside your five senses. Let nothing distract you. Walk in silence, eyes cast down, looking a yard or two in front of you. Attempt to walk through the mall and back again, touching no one, looking at no one, and disturbing nothing. Use your senses to tell you where people are, and avoid interaction. Because you can't look up, you will have to be acutely aware of what is coming toward you. But also, you will have to be aware of what is to your side and behind you. If people talk to you, ignore them.

Once you have completed this exercise successfully, go back the next Saturday and attempt the "advanced" course, which is to traverse the mall and back again with no one seeing you. You may consider it impossible—just walking through the mall—someone is bound to see. That is not so. Their eyes may look in your direction, but if your energy is centered within you and your thoughts and feelings tightly collected inside you, the composite of your body, thoughts, and emotions do not register on the attention of the passersby. How many times have you walked into a mall looking for a store and walked right past it? If you can miss a store, you can easily miss a crafty Warrior-Sage who is deliberately trying to hide from you.

Now, if one is serious about not being seen, then one would wear gray, preferably dark gray. It is not a color that projects much energy, so people don't notice it. Have you ever wondered why the various secret services of the world use gray cars? The fact is, if you buy a red car, everyone goes out of their way to hit it; if you buy a gray car, you melt into the background. So there you are in the mall wearing gray clothes, and you would choose a pair of soft shoes that don't "clank" as you walk. As you move through the mall, maintain a steady pace, for if you alter your step, people notice the change of rhythm.

Your line of sight should be set first horizontally out in front of you. Then dropped down 10 or 15 degrees so that you are looking ahead but slightly downwards. This way you'll be able to see if people notice you. Now here's the final trick. If you look at the passersby, they, in turn, will notice you, for in "looking" you transfer a part of your etheric to them and they feel it. What you have to do is allow "reality" in the mall to impact your sight without looking at it. Your sight-perception has to be "passive," not active. This ability to "see" without looking will be vital to you once you get into the etheric, for there, energy is moving so fast you don't have time to engage your consciousness in "looking." There you have to allow the etheric reality to touch you.

Finally, as you move through the mall in the Warrior-Sage mode, you hold a consciousness of nonjudgment and noncriticism so that none of your mind projects beyond you to the passersby. But more than nonjudgment, you develop the feeling of not even having an opinion about anything that you see in the mall. Nonjudgment is an "active" response, for you look at another and say, "I will not judge that." This engages your attention in "nonjudging." By training your mind in not having opinions, you become passive and receptive; you remain centered deep within yourself. Your mind perceives things and does not react in the slightest. In a way, this attitude becomes an affirmation of your absolute acceptance of life.

Once you are comfortable with accepting reality as it is, you can move about without others seeing you, for the impact you make on reality as you move is minimal. You step in the nonworld between normal reality and the etheric. You step beyond the perceptions of others to a world of your own.

Handy trick at customs, you might think, and you are right.

The only problem at the border post is that if you are carrying contraband and you exhibit the slightest emotion—if you have an opinion about it—the customs officer will nab you. You may wind up in the slammer, practicing your meditations in silence for quite some time. On the other hand, you may not. You may become very rich, very quickly.

Many years ago, I got a job as an advisor to a group of up-market smugglers. Good men and true they were, with very definite opinions as to their individuality. The Venezuelan government had an opinion, in those times, that a certain make of denim jeans should carry a 500 percent tariff. My employers, bless their little cotton socks, had a slightly different view. They felt that the indigenous population of those parts ought to be able to purchase jeans without getting stiffed by their government.

Now you may say that my friends were morally wrong, but who is to say that the opinion of a Mickey Mouse government official is more valid than the opinion of a gentleman smuggler. It was not as if the money collected by Venezuelan customs ever reached the people. My function for the group was to purchase the jeans in London, a perfectly legitimate act, and to arrange for their shipment to Curacao, a small island off the Venezuelan coast. From there the product was shipped to the mainland by boat—to be delivered into the hands of many a delighted customer a day or two later. I didn't stay at the job long enough to make a lot of money, but while in the group's employ, I learned the "psychology" of the trade and found the experiences valuable in understanding people and life. It helped me learn detachment and nonjudgment.

The wonderful thing about all the laws that the world insists on imposing on its people is that they allow the common folk a special "creativity" as they invent ingenious ways of getting around those laws. Their antics seem to me to be an exercise in simple forms of etheric invisibility. In my view—providing you are not hurting anyone—whatever your opinion is, is fine by me. I think it best for one to develop a creativity society approves of, but I can see the point of many disadvantaged people, who, suffering from a lack of opportunity and education, drift into a more twilight existence. Who am I to judge that?

Such a one was John—a man of about 50 who had struggled all his life to make ends meet doing worthless warehouse jobs in the East End of London. John scrimped and saved over 20 years and eventually bought a boat. He developed a small "travel agency" business offering conducted, scenic tours of the English Channel at night! His customers were gentlefolk from Pakistan who, desirous as they were of reaching England, and having heard back in Rawalpindi that Merry England was the place to be, were prepared to pay £1,500 for the benefit of John's safe and secure passage.

John loaded his customers on the Northern Coast of France near Boulogne and delivered them in robust good health at a small cove on the coast of Kent. After 18 months, John joined the middle class and bought a couple of small houses in Hillingdon. About that time, the local fuzz got wind of John's tours and paid him a visit. The cops in England are still very gentlemanly—they even call you "Sir" when they stop you for speeding. The sergeant of the local constabulary took John for a drink in a pub just off the Portobello road. He explained to my mate that the cops knew of John's enterprise but they couldn't prove it, and John, after a few drinks, sort of admitted to his part in the affair. The sergeant, a kindly man who was not above a little commerce himself, told John that if he did not quit, the cops would arrest him on a trumped-up charge that would ensure John's detention at the Queen's Pleasure for several years, but that if he quit, no more would be said of the matter. John's nautical days ended then and there.

What I learned from all these exotic characters was priceless to me, in metaphysical terms. First, I learned that once you don't judge or impose your morality on others, it sets you free emotionally. Second, I saw that in the nondescript lifestyles of these characters there was unusual freedom. Albeit their bent to criminality was, in the eyes of society, not to be approved of, yet within their criminality was a goodness—a fervor, an affirmation, perhaps, to redress some of the inequities of life. All of these characters had developed an invisibility stemming from society's alienation of them, and so they became detached. "Not belonging" allowed them a creative freedom that another, perhaps concerned about his social standing, involved as he might be in sustaining a position, does not possess.

It seems to me that the Warrior-Sage and the "twilight" people are not so very different. The detachment and secrecy of the criminal is motivated by his need to stay safe and to remain "outside" of society. The detachment of the Warrior-Sage is exactly the same, the only difference being that the criminal's alignment is negative, not wishing to be caught, and the Warrior-Sage is positive, not wishing to be "caught-up" in.

I learned as a young man that there is a special fluidity in nonattachment. Yet the whole of our education and programming brainwashes us into sustaining society. It forces us to remain within its clutches in order to sustain the status quo. It takes effort to push away from that and create the individual—detached and free. Emotionally, we are constantly suckered into having to belong, yet it takes only a little effort of mental agility to begin to feel more secure in not belonging. Try this the next time you hear two people discussing a problem: Let us say that one is asking the other the way to the bus station. Don't butt in even if you know the answer. Use the situation to train yourself to stay uninvolved. Now, if one of the two asks you, "Where's the bus station?" tell him. But if they don't ask, say nothing. What you are trying to learn is to become as little attached to events as possible. You are learning to stand to one side of the common reality. In becoming the silent observer, you gain a *Quickening*.

We teach our children in school to impress, to perform. "Who knows where the bus station is?" "I do, I do," and 50 hands go up. The mind of the child says, Let me prove that I am clever, that I have worth, that I am brighter than the others. As the Warrior-Sage, you are not going to mess with having to prove anything to anyone. You don't care if people think you are a complete idiot. In fact, you will generate that impression, somewhat as a smoke screen for your true power. The Mr. Magoo image of the bumbling fool who somehow manages to step off the roof just as a construction girder swings into place, is appropriate to the Warrior-Sage.

In the secrecy and silence of your "quest," you are looking to hide your power. People won't understand how you achieve the things you do. With the smoke screen, you reduce the threat to others. Your power, once consolidated, will frighten people. They will never be sure how much you know about them, and the more you know, the more often you will say nothing. You will constantly maneuver your troops to the high ground. There your energy rests, silent and unassailable.

If you are coming into power, avoid the pitfall of talking about it or of having to have people endorse or acknowledge it. That is a common weakness. It exposes you, dissipates the power, and leaves you uncertain of whether or not the power you feel is actually real. For example, many females nowadays have completed the process, started some years ago, of getting their power back from the males in their lives. This is a good move and just in time. If they don't take their power back, like right now, the next ten years will be a rocky path. But if a woman becomes overly aggressive, the baby goes out with the bathwater. The male retreats, and she loses a friend and possible helper.

Because people are weak, they always react to overt shows of strength. One doesn't want to generate negativity, especially when one is trying to get things done in a hurry. The Warrior-Sage, while not responding emotionally to the reactions of others, is, at the same time, the consummate diplomat. He knows what people want to hear, and he throws candies from the back of the truck to keep them happy. To achieve great things, one needs the support of others. The diplomat listens to the needs of others, some of which are expressed covertly, and then provides as best he can what the people want, when they want it, with minimum effort on his part.

One has to learn to be crafty. By crafty I don't mean sneaky or dishonest. It is more the craft of humanhood: understanding the world so totally and reading mechanical-man so completely that one knows what people want before they know what they want. It is only a matter of looking for the signs. I remember walking in a dense wood, as a child in England, with my father. After we had walked about an hour, I had no clue where we were. My father asked me, "Which way is north?" It was a cloudy day; I looked up for the sun and got no help. I did not know.

My father pointed in one direction and said, "That is north." He explained that the rain and moisture in England is blown over the Atlantic and arrives from the west. The moss on the tree is always on the wetside, or to the west of the trees. Knowing where west is, north is but a deduction. I remember thinking how clever that was. Life is full of moss on the wetside if you look for it.

A part of your craftiness is silence and secrecy. Again, by keeping silent you are not being covert. You are just being quiet. There is a tremendous difference between lying and not answering people's questions or inquiries too specifically. In the late sixties and early seventies, we were taught to share our feelings, and Gestalt therapy was all the rage. You remember the stuff: "I'm okay, you're okay, thank you for sharing it." We were taught the benefits of "putting it out there" and communicating to our nearest and dearest every little twang of the heart chakra.

I am not against communication, for it allows you to live in the truth when relating to others. It's also very helpful on your climb up the energy ladder from confusion to consolidation. However, once you have it together, there will be many parts of your life that you will never talk about. You will deal with individuals on a "need to know" basis only.

Besides the need to hide your power, there is another good reason for keeping your methods to yourself. Have you ever wondered why the European occult brotherhoods always had secrecy as a pivotal point of their philosophy? There were several reasons. First, in the olden days, the Christians tried to maneuver themselves into a monopoly over magical practices; the Roman Catholic mass is a prime example. As they struggled for supremacy over the minds of the people, they naturally outlawed the competition. Anyone chipping away at the monopoly was persecuted, given a hard time, and/or killed.

The negativity of the more "wacko" Christian cults is still prevalent today. It is a body of psychic antagonism 2,000 years old that assails anyone who doesn't accept their principles. I don't mean to imply that all Christian sects are similar. There are many, in fact, that are holy and good and serve an honorable function. But there are as many others that sustain a tribal neurosis antagonistic to an individual's freedom. That neurosis is a part of the "collective unconscious" and can be harmful to you. Silence, a noncombative attitude, and the smoke screen are your keys.

Further, on an energy level, silence allows you to make use of "psychic tension." As you conceive an idea in your mind, its strength lies in the correlation between the amount of concentration you have given the thought, the level of emotion you exert around it (either positive or negative), and the way you feel about the thought—that is, whether you consider it a fantasy/daydream or a reality.

There are other factors that empower your thoughts, but for the moment, center on the fact that each thought is contained in a casing of electromagnetic power. Imagine it as a molecule containing your special thought. The tension in that molecule builds up as you center on the thought and empower it. The thought is stored in your memory, and it begins to lose power if you do not concentrate upon it from time to time. It also loses power if you harass it. You can overconcentrate on something.

As the vitality of the thought builds and begins to swamp your entire being, your whole energy changes and you begin to pull correspondences from reality—events that match the thought, which have the same feeling or correspondence within them. If you break silence and talk about your thoughts, you release the psychic tension in the molecule. By living through the idea in your words, you engage your feelings. So your mind, which does not differentiate between fantasy and reality, is actually living and breathing the event while you talk. Once the event is "lived," most of its psychic tension is released. That is why when you feel uncomfortable or experience fear, it helps to discuss it with another.

As you develop power and start to use your mind to deliver life to you, a dramatic change takes place. Instead of waking into daily life and haphazardly experiencing whatever is there, reality comes and gets you. You bend space and time, pulling to you the reality you require. You will not want to dissipate what may amount to months of effort in one silly conversation. Keeping the most important things to yourself allows you to work on them without distraction.

The other reason for secrecy and silence is that in silence, there is mystery. I talked about this at length in *Affirmations*. Now I will simply say that mystery grants additional impact and power. The reality you have taken within you becomes more real. Others project into that reality. First, they cannot destroy what is there because they are ignorant of it. Second, they grant you a power that perhaps you do not as yet have. It helps you. By keeping the world guessing, you are always one step ahead of the program, and people find it difficult to put their finger on who and what you are. Therefore, they can't stick you in a box.

7

BENDING TIME, WATCHING EVERYTHING, MISSING NOTHING

IN SILENCE you enter into a timelessness that allows you to comprehend the "unreal" world of the etheric. It is the first step to your penetrating that etheric. To do this, you will have to start to bend time. This is important because the etheric is timeless. Events occur in sequence but not in time. This sounds illogical, but in the etheric it is not. There is a feeling that one event comes before the other, but there is a dreamy, timeless quality to events. Naturally, in our world, an atomic second is an atomic second. But it is in how you perceive that second that the bending takes place.

To the logical mind, time is linear. So one feels that the future is not yet created, and we get the impression that what we experience in life is a factor of chance. But that is an illusion. In fact, time and our future experiences stand around us. They are composed of thought and exist in the present in varying degrees of psychic intensity. That is why a visionary can perceive an event before it actually takes place. What he or she sees is the thought-form of the event prior to its transfer from thought into reality.

In effect, what comes to you and at what speed it arrives is regulated by the inner you in your subconscious. The illusion is sustained because the subconscious is hidden from you so your waking intellect is not usually aware of what messages you are putting out from deep within. The logical mind experiences circumstances that it does not understand, and it feels that the sequence of events that make up its reality are haphazard. This occurs because the intellect often has a completely different opinion or view than does the inner subconscious mind.

In fact, your position in time is controllable and fluid. Not only can you bend your perception of time (how long things take), but you can control the speed at which those things come at you. For a year I worked in an Italian restaurant as a helper in the kitchen. We had two chefs. The regular chef worked five nights a week, the other, the remaining two nights. The regular guy was a model of order and discipline, and when he worked, customers arrived at a steady pace and meals were delivered promptly. The other chef was a basket case. He was always screaming and shouting; things flew in all directions, and I was constantly picking spaghetti off the ceiling. I noticed that when he worked, the customers arrived in bunches. It would be deathly quiet, and then suddenly 30 orders would come down the hatch all at once. The kitchen went into an Italian version of a Chinese fire drill. It was not a pretty sight. The contrast between the two chefs made me realize that the disciplined, ordered guy was in fact somehow controlling the flow of customers, whereas his replacement did not.

You can probably see this in your life. When you are out of balance, the psychic tension that holds everything around you in its proper place snaps, time breaks down, and events rush at you in a headlong frenzy. This occurs because the etheric composure and strength you normally sustain deteriorate with imbalance, so your protection is lost. Events take on an erratic flow, and you seem to be at the mercy of chance.

To establish control over time, you first have to slow it down. This is accomplished by balance, by living more and more in the now, by having fewer and fewer thoughts about the future and the past, and by disengaging from thinking about how long things take or about what time it is. It is helpful not to lock your life into time schedules. It is too easy to develop a life that is so regimented that you are just "tick-tocking" through it like a wind-up toy. We decide when things ought to occur, and if they are late, we get upset.

Allow things to happen whenever they happen so you develop a lifestyle that has as little mechanical rhythm as possible. Breaking up the rigid patterns helps to elongate time. Go to sleep at different times, have lunch at three in the morning, and so forth. Meditation of the theta kind will also help the elongation process.

Here's an exercise you can try. Get into a deep meditative level, but keep your eyes open. You will want your eyes to focus a foot or two away from you, at a downward angle of 45 degrees. Have in front of you a clock that has a secondhand. Watch the seconds as the hand rotates around the clock, and place your feelings at the spot between the "ticks" as it moves forward. At first, the spaces between each second will seem fairly normal, but as you stare at the clock, the time-space between the "clicks" becomes greater. Eventually, it will seem to you that the space has become infinite, and you may on occasions wonder if the clock has stopped. It will seem that the secondhand takes endless time between one position and the next.

As the *Quickening* becomes a part of your life, you will have the impression that time is slowing down. Also, it will seem to take on a spatial quality. It will feel as if time has become "wider" and your life richer. It is true that time also slows down when you go through a very negative experience. This is because when engaged in negative emotions, you pull your etheric web into concave waves of energy that have a way of condensing and compacting your life force. Your energy is tighter. That tightness creates the feeling that time has slowed down and that your negative experience is taking forever. The compacting of time in negativity is a totally different experience from the slowing of time that takes place in the *Quickening*. The negativity is uncomfortable, whereas the *Quickening* has a surreal, eternal feeling to it.

The main trick to stopping time is feeling that you have enough of it. Whenever you do not feel this way, it is always a factor in your lack of balance and organization. As you begin to bend your perception of time, you also enter into an understanding that there is almost no limit to how much you can do in any given period of time. If you can bring your mind into turbo-thought, you can physically gloss over events such as a stone skipping a lake. You touch each item only minimally. You enter into a style of living that is very unusual. It allows maximum penetration with minimum effort. Results flow at such speed that your belief patterns crack before the rhythm does. As soon as you doubt your ability to sustain the speed at which you are operating, your performance slows down again. You enter once more into sluggish normal time. It takes practice to hold a concentrated turbo-thought, but it can be done. I'll explain all that in the chapters on the etheric.

It is enough to say at this point that stopping time is a vital first step, and you have to work on it vigorously or you will find the other techniques out of your reach. Once you feel you have mastered your ability to maneuver time, then you will want to expand your awareness within time. The trick is to inspire yourself to concentrate more and more on life. So the total experience you get increases. As it does, you will have the sensation of time's being "fuller" and, therefore, slower. Life will seem more in control and less will slip away from you.

By training your mind to look at the minute details of life, you force it to become more perceptive. In addition, noticing everything helps you to develop peripheral perception, and it forces you to stay awake. Try picking up a stone and looking at it for several minutes. Notice everything there is to be discovered about that stone—its shape, smell, indentations, weight, and so forth. Next, try to put yourself inside that stone and become it— listen for the silence within it. What depth of silence do you perceive is there?

Then pick a flower and stare at it until you become aware that within the flower there is an entire universe as complex as our own. Demand of your mind that it notice everything and that it remember everything and keep you informed at all times. It certainly has the capacity. It is just programmed to be lazy and to remember only a few facts that are important, and often it does not even manage to remember them successfully. Why operate through the physical at half-speed? Insist on more, and you'll get it.

You can invent exercises for yourself that will help train your mind so that it knows that you demand it to receive and remember even the most trivial information. Watch a short video clip, and have a friend ask you questions about what occurred. Or listen to a friend's conversation, and while the person is talking, notice every move he makes. Be aware of his change of posture, and notice around what remarks those changes occur. Demand of your mind that nothing, absolutely nothing, be missed.

Finally, in learning to bend time, it's helpful to practice getting a little out ahead of time. This is achieved by beginning to anticipate (not guess) what is going to happen next. The way to do this is to train your intuitive feelings to read the energy of a situation so you know what will happen next. The more you ask of your inner mind, the more it gets used to having that information ready for you. Ask at least 10 to 15 times a day and believe the answers you get, even if you are wrong at times.

For example, when a person is talking to you, anticipate their next few words, then anticipate their next sentence, and so on. In a given situation, decide how the pattern will unfold before it does. Watch people in a supermarket, say, and ask your intuition to decide which aisle they will turn down or what product they will reach for. By your constant asking, your inner mind gets used to the idea that this practice is important to you, and you will flex your mind to greater and greater strength.

You may ask, "Isn't this exercise going to pull me into future-thought and away from the present?" It does not. Future-thought is your mind's putting you ahead into a future fantasy. This exercise asks you to read the current energy and decide where it will develop in the future—that is, is the person going to turn down the left aisle or the right? In other words, you are pulling the future to you from current information, rather than projecting yourself forward into it. There is a vast difference.

I was sitting in the south of France on the beach at Cagnes Sur Mer. Traveling with me was a hairy little occultist I had met in Paris several weeks previously. He was a shabby little man with a fully paid-up membership in the "Struggles Club." Yet he had a vast knowledge and a fine wit, and so his company, although expensive, was entertaining and illuminating. There on the beach he looked ludicrously out of place. He wore a crumpled wool suit with his trousers rolled up to his knees, and a knotted handkerchief on his head. Beside him was a bottle of beer ceremoniously placed as flagpole on a mound of sand. We sat talking about the occult and the hidden power of the mind, when during the conversation he asked me to notice a French family that was busy creating a picnic nearby.

He would pick a member of the family and ask me what they

were going to do next. At first, I would try guessing. I was invari-
ably wrong. He directed me away from intellect into intuition,
and to my amazement, I could give him exact answers. We played
this game for about 40 minutes, during which he would embell-
ish the scene by telling me intimate details about each of the characters, about how they felt about the day, and their attitude toward
life. The family rose to begin a game of Frisbee, and their dog,
who had been sitting nearby, began barking with the excitement
of events. My little hairy occultist told me to use my mind to stop
the dog's barking. How? I asked.

He explained that all animals and humans alike are an intrusion into the etheric web of the earth, and that, although the dog's
etheric is weaker than the overall etheric web of the planet at any
given point, nevertheless the concentrated etheric around the dog
was, in fact, stronger. He explained that this forces the etheric of
the planet to be displaced in order to accommodate the dog's. At
the point of displacement, there is a very slight invisible gap
where the etheric web of the dog pushes the etheric of the earth
away. That gap, explained my friend, is the gateway into the non-
world. It is also the access point into the etheric of the animal.

My penniless occult friend told me to run my mind up the
spine of the dog and to hold my attention at a point on the dog's
head. He told me to place, with my mind's eye, my left hand
under the dog's neck in the area of the voice box and to put the
other hand on top of the dog's head. The upper hand was to be a
light and friendly touch as if I were stroking the dog, the lower
hand, firm and insistent. "Now," he said, "capture the dog with
your mind and surround the dog's head with your energy so that
whatever visual distractions the dog may have are obliterated by
the force of your mental grip."

I began to hold the dog as instructed and immediately felt an
energy draining from me. I realized that I did not have the power
to hold the dog for long. It was as if a part of me was being used

up in the effort. I could feel a pulling sensation on my solar plexus, which gave me a slight feeling of nausea. A battle was taking place between the inherent desire of the dog to bark, and my will, which forbade it. For the first few seconds, the dog was unaffected by my grip, but then the cadence of its bark changed, becoming less insistent, and, within 30 seconds, it had descended through several whimpers into silence. I held the dog in my grip for about 20 seconds, and then it broke free and started barking again.

I asked my friend if that meant I had failed. He replied, "No," explaining that the dog's inherent will to bark in that situation was as strong as its need to breathe, and that eventually it would break through.

That night the hairy occultist borrowed the equivalent of $200 from me, saying that he had to go to Nice on some urgent business and that he would return with my cash in two days. That was the last I saw of him. In retrospect, my investment was reasonable. You pay to know what you think!

By constantly going into your inner mind to ask for information about events that have not as yet happened, you train it to "read" the energy patterns of life. Thus, you move from intellect and guesswork to intuition and feeling. Eventually, you will become so accurate at reading patterns that you almost always know what is going to happen before it does. At that point, you have begun to step from this world to straddle another.

THE ETHERIC
NON-WORLD

S PEAKING OF the non-world or other dimensions, have you ever
wondered where the spirit world is? You read stories in the
Bible about J. C. ascending into heaven. Where did he go? Did he
fly off to Mars, or what? People talk in terms of communication
with the spirit world, but where do all these things exist? Is your
spirit guide between your ears, or is it standing at your left shoul-
der near the fridge? Does it hover someplace between the earth
and nowhere?

Again, these inconsistencies bothered me, for in all the teachings I have read, no one ever explained where the inner worlds
actually were. When I lived in England, it seemed to me that people there were very knowledgeable about spirit communication
and psychic phenomena. Perhaps it's because 90 percent of all
ghosts seem to live in England. God knows why; I am told it's the
damp. Belief in the spirit world forms a part of the national her-

itage. In fact, any decent lord who does not hover around the battlements for at least 500 years after his death is considered a bit suspect, having prematurely deserted his subjects. But when I posed my awkward-brat questions as to the location of these inner worlds, I was always met with evasive answers. "Have a cup of tea, Dearie."

In death and in the out-of-body experience, the first change that takes place is that a portion of your etheric, which also contains the inherent memory of your personality, disengages from the body. At that stage it hovers in the room. So it seems to me that a part of the inner worlds are right here, but beyond normal perception. In stage two, the wraith of the etheric moves down a tunnel into other dimensions of consciousness. Because these experiences are subjective, the tunnel is sometimes described as a hole in a wall, a gate, or even a cave, but it is an "entering in."

Often the tunnel is described as containing a rush of wind. This, I believe, is because the tunnel is not in fact a tube, but rather two energies twisted around each other—helix shaped. One energy flowing into our dimension, the other flowing out, and the tube or tunnel is the area up the center of these two forces. I don't think the sensation people feel is, in fact, wind. I surmise that it is a flow of electromagnetic force and that the flow is translated as "wind" by a mind used to physical sensations.

Note also that I don't say "up" and "down" the tube. It is natural, in a Judeo-Christian society, to be predisposed to think of heaven as celestial and "up," and hell as opposite and therefore "down." They are not. It is a mistake to think so. In fact, generally speaking, the tunnel is more or less horizontal, the inner worlds at the other end being "across" from us. So if Jesus did anything, he "slid across" to heaven, like making home plate rather than "ascending."

Moot point, perhaps. But I like things as accurate as possible, and the Bible never mentions exactly where he went. Imagine the circumstances: You've been hanging around with this incredibly mystical character, the Son of God, for three years. The rotten Romans and their capitalist lackey, Pilate, knock off your guru one Friday afternoon. Suddenly, three days later, joy! joy! There's ya' man, walking about in the suburbs, right as rain. But before you have time to say, "By your leave, Sire, and how's your father?" he up and drifts off into the clouds.

Now, was the question on everybody's lips, "When does the pub open?" Heck no. They would have had to have asked, "Where did he go? Will he be back in a minute with a lei from Hawaii or what? What the hell's going on?" In the Bible, no one sorted that one out. I suppose the folk gathered at the event forgot to ask. Perhaps God wasn't up to telling them, or maybe the Gospelers were too thick to understand the explanation anyway. Most likely, the event never occurred, and the writers were just copying down the stories of the "death of the initiate" and his three-day journey in the inner worlds that they had gotten from the priests of the Pyramid in Egypt. I don't know; I don't have an answer, but I do know the story left me hanging somewhat. In passing, and nothing to do with any of the tube stuff, let me tell you my favorite Jesus story. Now before I do, if you are a heavyweight, dyed-in-the-wool Christian you may not like this story one bit, so jump down a paragraph, and pick up the text there.

Jesus was camped with his disciples on the banks of the Galilee. He turned to them and said, "Who do the people say I am?" There was silence for a moment, then one of the disciples who had majored in philosophy at the University of Somewhere replied, "Sire, you are the eschatological manifestation of the groundwork of our being, the kerygma of which gives meaning to our interpersonal relationships." To which Jesus replied, "Yer what?"

Enough of this frivolity! On with the show. Back to the tube and the location of the spirit world. We talked about the sensation of wind in the tunnel, and there are only two other things I have to add. First, the tunnel seems to me to have a bend in it. I don't know why this is so; I can only surmise that some force is bending it. In the same way that light is bent around stars with large gravitational fields, there is some force acting on the outside of the tube that bends it. Maybe it is the gravitational field of our earth.

Second, I have never been able to figure out how far it is from our end of the tube (the physical world) to the other end of the tube (the spirit worlds). The trip "up" takes no more than a few seconds; it feels instantaneous. The difficulty is that with having no external terms of reference (all you see is the inside of the tube), there is no way you can accurately tell how fast you are going. You can, in fact, move your imagination faster than the speed of light so in those few seconds you may move a vast distance. On the other hand, in the inner worlds, space and time take on a different quality, and the whole question of distance becomes obsolete.

The other difficulty is that the myriad of dimensions available at the other end of the tube do not have signposts, so you are never quite sure of your exact location. You judge the location by the way it "feels," but there is no sign that says, "Heaven welcomes careful drivers."

Another point that has to be looked at before we can answer the question "Where is the spirit world?" is: Is there just one tube, or are there many? It is a fact that no matter where you are on earth, the tube is always there. Two people dying instantaneously in, say, Alaska and Australia, both see the tube right there almost at once. Neither travels to the other's location. So we are looking at either one vast tube covering the whole earth, which you can enter from anywhere, or we're looking at a lot of tubes.

The vast tube theory is not my favorite, because the tube does not seem that large. When moving along the tube, you can see the sides. So now we are left with the idea of lots of tubes. One for each person, perhaps? An alternative idea is that the etheric of the earth is riddled with tubes, that there may be, in fact, trillions of them all very close together. So no matter where you have your out-of-body experience or death, there you find a tube.

Another interesting feature is that there are many different locations in the spirit world at the end of the tube. But while traveling up the tube, one does not seem to make turns or detours. Your destination is decided by you, or by the inner you, before you actually leave the physical dimension. This would give added weight to the idea of many tubes. For if there is just one big tube, in order for one to reach various locations, one would be forced to make turns.

Here's my theory: The etheric around your body is made up of exactly the same substance as the etheric around the earth, except it is more dense. Your etheric is made up of energy flowing in and out and contains the same helix shapes, so there are tubes in the center of each of them. When exiting the body, your energy flows from your feet up to the crown chakra.

Interestingly enough, in the bi-location phenomenon, where the physical body is moved over a distance across the earth instantaneously, the energy has to be set up correctly at the feet, and as it gains momentum, it rolls up the body. The physicalness of the body folds into itself as sand going from one end of an hourglass to the other. Once the vibration reaches the waistline, the transfer is on, and there is no turning back. Where you go depends on the power of your concentration as the vibration hits critical velocity and intensity. The reason why many don't understand this phenomenon is because they think in terms of traveling from, say, London to Chicago. They don't understand how a physical body could be moved across such a distance in less than a minute. In fact, you don't "travel to" your intended location. As the energy hits the critical stage, the etheric of the location that you are concentrating on "comes and gets you." That is all I can say at present, but if you have been tooling around with these ideas, getting nowhere, you now at least have an alternative tack from which to approach them.

The reason the energy flows from the feet up is because the lower chakras are moving at a slower pace than the crown. Once the oscillations of the brain are no longer creating the electromagnetic field that holds the etheric in—because one is either in trance or dead—the energy is naturally attracted to the fastest-moving center in the body, which is why you don't exit through your armpit.

It seems to me that the mini-tubes in your etheric are automatically connected through a correspondence of some kind to the tubes in the etheric of the earth. Perhaps the mini-tubes in the etheric of the body are the ends of some of the other tubes. Anyway, your energy flows up through the body along these lines and out of the crown chakra. It then picks up one of the earth tubes and flows along that.

In looking at all of this over a period of time, I came to the conclusion that the entire physical universe of stars is just part of one nucleus, and that the nucleus is inside a larger molecule that we call the spirit world, somewhere near its center. There may well be other physical universes inside other spirit world molecules. Our physical universe of stars is just the center core of the molecule, and the core is surrounded by the rest of the molecule, which is less dense. The rest is what we call the spirit world.

This would mean that the spirit world interlaces the physical and is all around it. I draw this conclusion from the fact that the gateway to the spirit world is right here on earth, but because of the spirit world's vastness, it is also all around the universe and beyond. The expanding physical universe of stars is expanding within itself, being as it is within the Life Force or etheric energy that surrounds it, what we call the spirit world. This means, in effect, that the universe has no beginning and no end. At the point in space of the farthest expansion of the universe where physical matter ends, there is the etheric Life Force of the leading galaxy, still inside the cone. That etheric is no more or less matter than gas or rock. It may be more rarefied, but it still is wave-motion, as is the rock. The Big Bang Theory postulates that the universe exploded and that all the galaxies hurtled away from each other. At some point, the velocity of that explosion will be spent, and the galaxies will cease to expand; eventually, the universe will collapse back on itself.

If you imagine the cone of Life Force that we call the spirit world from an overview, you would see that the physical universe is expanding inside the cone. A human looking from within the confines of the oscillation of the brain would feel that there was a definite leading edge to the universe. But if your perspective changed and you were on the outside of the universe and beyond the cone, you would see the universe at its center expanding and contracting, and you would see that the physical universe was of the same Life Force stuff as the spirit worlds that surround it. So you would conclude that the physical universe has no beginning and no end. You would just observe it moving within itself. It is and it always has been. Then the idea of a Supreme Creator some-how molding the rock on Monday changes.

Mathematical graphs of black holes look exactly the same as the cone. Perhaps those holes in space are just areas where mat-ter is moving from one part of the cone to another, undergoing change as it leaves our physical universe and reenters the etheric of the spirit world in a more rarefied form of antimatter. The black hole, then, is exactly like the tubes in the etheric that con-nect us to the cone, except that perhaps it connects our universe with even more vast molecules of other cones or spirit worlds and other universes.

The conclusion I reach is that the spirit world is conical in shape. It is impossible to get beyond or on the outside of the etheric web of the spirit worlds to confirm this. But the bend in the tube and the curved lines of force that exist in the etheric certainly give the impression that it is cone-shaped. The universe as we know it, is near the center of the cone.

Does that mean that at death you fly off to Mars? No, you are entering into the cone, part of which is around Mars, but as you enter the cone, other factors come into play. While the etheric exists around Mars, it does not contain any human emotional influence. If I say to you, "Go sit on a rock in the desert for 90 years," it won't sound really attractive to you, which is why at death we don't shoot off to Mars. Because we are used to life on earth, the spirit worlds we inhabit are close to, or within, that part of the earth's etheric that contains the emotional thought-forms of humans. If you could stand at a point several hundred miles above the earth's surface and look back at the earth's etheric, you would see within it the emanations of nature, but also you would see the hopes and aspirations of man.

Each thought-form that leaves the human body ends up traveling a certain distance within the earth's etheric, and that gives the etheric of the earth human qualities. Although our planet seems to be a lifeless rock hurtling through space, it is in fact an individualized evolution that exists inside its own etheric web. You can think of it as a Higher Self, which rather than taking on human form, has accepted the entire planet as its body or vehicle for its evolution. It has a mind of its own. It is the sum total of everything here, and in addition it is the sum total of whatever energy is projected into its etheric by humans. In the same way as your etheric contains all your characteristics and thought-forms, it also contains and is affected by the thoughts and feelings of others.

The earth regulates its own balance naturally, making adjustments for changing conditions and various changes in human attitudes and actions. The etheric web of the earth, therefore, contains the emotions of man as one of its features. As one's consciousness enters the etheric web of the earth, at death it naturally seeks correspondences it recognizes. So it drifts to a part of the etheric that reflects its emotional/spiritual position. From that I conclude that the spiritual worlds we call "heaven and hell" must be close to or within the influence of the earth. But don't make the mistake of thinking that I mean that heaven hovers 50 miles up. What I mean is that, because heaven is "inner," it is within the etheric influence of the earth, but you can't think of it geographically. You have to identify its position by the intrinsic fellowship of its consciousness. The group-mind collected around itself creates the location. If everyone simultaneously changed their mind, the location of heaven would change, also. But the fact that the spirit world definitely interlaces the physical is, I believe, evidence that wherever the spirit world's location, emotionally and geographically, it has to be close.

It seems to me that once our Higher Self began its descent into the influence of the earth plane, the part of it that separated and descended lost velocity or intensity in that descent. It is only through completing the earth experience through various incarnations that it gains enough power to eventually make the climb back out of the emotional influence of earth and humanhood into more rarefied parts of the cone. The emotions of humanity and the slowness at which the speed of the human condition oscillates create a gravitational pull that entraps the Higher Self.

When you die and enter into whatever part of the cone you are pulled to, let us say that you have entered a liberated, expansive, spiritual part of the cone—what we would call heaven. There you begin to see yourself in the light of the God-Force, and gradually your opinion of yourself would change. You would no longer see yourself so much as a personality with a name, characteristics, and opinions, but rather, as the ego melts, you would see yourself as a part of the divine whole. That part has an individualized identity. It is you. But it also knows itself to be a part of the whole. That knowledge grants it spiritual honor.

If, then, you visited those parts of the spirit world that man calls "hell," you would see that the individuals there were not affected by the Light of God, and so they would still hold to their earthbound ego/personalities. Unrestrained by physical limitations, the restrictive opinions, self-serving traits, and manipulative ways of those found there would be heightened. Their dimension, which is created by, and reflects their attitudes, would exhibit all those undesirable properties. It would look to you to be dead. Very likely you would be repulsed by the ugliness of the people and their attitudes, which would be clearly in view all around them.

Observing this dimension of hell, you would be surprised to realize that those found there did not consider the dimension ugly. In fact, although they would seem to you troubled and perhaps evil, you could see from their actions and feelings that they gained a certain pleasure in sustaining their infringing, restrictive world.

You could see also that the totality of what they were, created the dimension they lived in, that in fact there is no judgment after death. One cannot, in the rarefied etheric of the spirit world, hide what one actually is. Thus, a person of little energy, fearful and weak, finds himself in a dimension that is insecure and little permeated by the God-Force. If you are strong and assured and you have already developed a powerful, uncluttered alignment to the God-Force, you would wind up in a dimension that has no restriction at all, where the God-Force shines with an intensity that is exquisite.

The Life Force etheric that is a part of you now, in the human body, is the same Life Force, or God-Force, that you will experience in the cone as you enter the spirit world. That means that a part of you exists in many dimensions of consciousness. Meaning, you are already in a heaven or hell right now. A part of you exists in eternity. That part is inside your inner mind and is subjugated by the ego/personality and the inhibition created by the brain. But it is there.

As you develop your quest toward the energy of the Warrior-Sage, the ego melts as it would in the spirit world. Then, climbing as you do out of the restrictive aspects of life, the light shines upon that eternal spark within you, and it gains strength. The domination of the ego/personality is eventually diminished, although never broken completely. But as your quest gains momentum, you begin, while still on earth, to enter the divine whole. It means that when you die, you will spend only a brief moment, if any at all, in those parts of the cone that most people arrive at after death.

There will be no need for you to experience the melting of the ego or your reunification with God, for you will already have achieved that while still alive on earth. So, we arrive at the crux of the Warrior-Sage's identity, his modus operandi if you like. He sees himself gradually melting as a personality, and he accepts its death as such, for he knows it is the only way for him to proceed. The lessons of earth having been learned, he is left with either existing in a vapid, spent life that offers little of interest or learning, or he has to allow himself to let go and to cast his fate in an unknown spiritual dimension that he finds he now straddles.

The conflict of this decision is what holds most people back. It is not a move lightly taken. There is always a hesitancy. It takes the courage of the Warrior to even attempt it. That is why, as a part of the *Quickening,* I stress the importance of getting out of mechanical-man's survival mentality into a Warrior's detachment about his death. It gets the ego used to the idea that eventually it will melt. As you develop the uncluttered philosophy that the *Quickening* requires, you enter a dimension of consciousness that is more akin to heaven than hell. That is why I can say that such attitudes will eventually liberate your spirit. It is not just a psychological process of empowerment; it is also a process of spiritual development.

Some might say that I am a little harsh on the institutional religions, but again there is much within their teachings that is diametrically opposed to your spiritual growth. All the dogma and the strutting and the bizarre claims the churches make are just manifestations of an insecure ego-cult. You don't need too much of that before you are trussed up like a Christmas turkey. The God-Force is liberating, not confining. To align to that divinity within you, you have to take on its properties. You become Godlike, not holy-moly. You create, right or wrong, a philosophy that's yours. That philosophy might be adapted from one you borrowed, but it has to have your ideals and views at its center.

Now you may say, "But I like the church and its teachings; help me, I feel comfortable in its society." And I would say, "Fine, who am I to mess with that?" But I would ask that you consider internalizing your religion, making it occult, making it yours. I would also ask that you not let anyone dictate to you from within that philosophy what it is that you should do and what it is that you should feel and say.

Further, you cannot accept a true spirituality if you do not grant yourself direct access to the Force. For if you don't, that becomes an affirmation that you do not feel strong enough to approach the God-Force in your own right. If you are operating solely through an institution, it is like having an agent that represents you to yourself. That is not fully empowering. So a Christian would dump much of the "twaddle" and take to his heart the idea of the Christ Consciousness. He would endorse quietly within the privacy of his prayers, the freedom of the Christ Consciousness, the liberation, the love that was offered. The Christian Warrior-Sage would not truck for one moment with any dogma of guilt, nor would he accept any of the petty maneuvers of the church. When he heard them claiming to be chosen or to be the only church endorsed by God, he would disassociate himself from that, realizing that their claim came out of insecurity and a feeling of self-importance. Eventually, the Warrior would develop a more divine version of his religion that allows him complete freedom. But it is hard for the mind of man to disengage from the programming. It is deep.

That is why you may find yourself on the wall of the prison looking out, but you may not jump immediately. There is hesitation in giving up all that you are used to and trusting in the unseen forces that you are only now becoming familiar with. But when you do, your need to be on the earth plane ceases. The lessons are learned, and your energy is now bigger than life. This does not mean that your incarnation is necessarily over. You may live on many years. But although your body remains in the physical world till death, your consciousness exists for the most part in a spiritual etheric world, and it is there that you will study and learn new lessons although still alive on earth. Once that etheric beachhead is established, you gain energy quickly, and soon you will know that you are finished here, that there is no reason to fear; for once this life is over, you will never have to come back.

If you accept Buddhist and Hindu tenets, it would seem that we spend endless incarnations toiling on the wheel of misfortune, seeking to become holy enough to leave. You can stuff that in your ear! It's just not accurate. In 500 B.C. there was nothing to do, life crawled along at a snail's pace, folk lived for 25 to 30 years and then "plopped over" for no explainable reason. Their lives were at the mercy of fate, and misery and misfortune were commonplace. It's natural that philosophers in those times would presume that nothing much ever changed, that it would take a thousand incarnations for you to transcend circumstances. You can see how the ancients came up with the wheel of misfortune routine. But then they had never seen a Boeing 747 or a postage stamp. The idea of a newspaper headline traveling on a laser beam, 42,000 miles in under a second, would have been beyond them.

They could not possibly have understood the speed at which things move today. Just think of how much you have learned in the last few years and what experiences you have acquired. You may feel that you have completed several incarnations already in this life. Then, if you consider what you still have to learn, it probably won't amount to much. Many people feel that the lessons of earth are not so difficult to grasp. You don't have to be an expert to transcend the physical; you only have to experience it and understand it. If you spend a month in France, you get the flavor of France, you grasp the experience, and the *inner you* has done France. You don't have to meet every Frenchman there is or read all the books in French literature to get it. It is the same with your spiritual evolution. The idea of coming back a thousand times makes no sense in the light of modern experience.

Another point about reincarnation that has captured my thought is: Does everyone have the same number of incarnations, or do some Higher Selves pass through the earth experience quickly while others take longer? Is it possible that a high-speed spirit could wrap its evolution on the earth plane in just one existence, thus eliminating the need to reincarnate at all? It's certainly true of life to say that some people burn along at a fierce racket, while others proceed more slowly. An incarnation in 1000 B.C. would not have afforded the same range of possibilities as an incarnation today. But whatever the case, you are right now at the quintessence of your spiritual development, and you have the opportunity to wrap and pack the final conclusion within this lifetime. That is exciting: a quest, a dream, a possibility never before offered, to be accepted in humility and courage, or to be missed.

ETHERIC
MANEUVERS

A S I DEVELOPED my quest, I searched, as you have, through all
the various teachings available. I found many helpful, but
what they did for me was assist me in becoming more efficient
within tick-tock—few of the teachings really showed me how to
get out of tick-tock.

In other parts of this book, we look at the psychology of the
Quickening and the stance of the Warrior-Sage. Now I want to
talk a while about etheric strengthening. This, more than anything, helped me break out of tick-tock and penetrate the inner
worlds so that I could learn more than what is available in the
ordinary way of things.

The hard part of trying to write about the etheric is that it is
only a feeling. The ideas do not drop easily into logic. One finds
oneself fishing for words to describe things that one knows on an
inner level, but that resist a written explanation.

The etheric is the true world. Your physical body and the planet are a solid manifestation of the etheric, but in the end, all that you are is the etheric web. When I said that you are already in the spirit world, what I meant was that you are etheric and that the spirit world is etheric, so you exist simultaneously in a myriad of other dimensions as well as the physical. The Warrior's secret is that he knows this, and he uses it to facilitate his life.

When you look at another being, what you are really looking at is an etheric web that is imprinted upon by thought-form and feeling. That person is not usually aware of his true reality. He or she sees the physical as the only option. In the etheric, your ability to move and create is a millionfold more free and expansive.

The first move is to begin to oscillate your etheric web and to move it around. I am going to give you three exercises that expand and move the etheric so that it becomes more viable. Normally a person's etheric web is stiff and sticky, and it only moves as a reaction to emotions. If it is projected, it is usually done without the person's intent or knowledge, and as it travels away from the person's body, it has a spasticity to it, for normally it never moves that far away.

What we are looking to achieve here is, first, you have to know that the etheric exists. There is an exercise that I included on one of my audiocassettes that will help you. It involves looking at the etheric of a tree at dusk. I don't want to repeat it here, but if you turn to page 147, it will be there. Second, we begin by manipulating the etheric to allow it to take on more Life Force and, so, become more viable. Think of it as a sticky film of transparent mist that surrounds your body. At first it is like dough. As you move and knead that dough, it becomes lighter, faster, and more flexible.

First Etheric Move: The Stretch

Variations of this exercise are commonly used by students of the out-of-body experience as a way of developing elasticity in the etheric. You perform it lying down north-to-south, with your head to the north. Get into a meditative state and relax your body. Start by visualizing a wheel hovering at the end of your feet. Have the wheel turn counterclockwise, then run the wheel up and down your body so that your body is in the center of the wheel. Do this ten times.

Now put your mind at the area of your crown chakra and run around your body, delineating it at a distance of a quarter of an inch. Go on the outside of your body, then along the inside of your thighs and up the other side. When you get to the crown chakra once more, rest. Then visualize a hook that is attached to the crown. Imagine it pulling you backwards, and see how far you can create that pull. Stop, rest, then pull again. Repeat this four or five times.

Now run your mind down to your feet, and elongate your legs so that in your mind's eye they are three feet longer than normal. Sustain a concentration at the new position of your feet so that you can really feel that your legs are now a yard longer. Next, run up to the crown and elongate your body through your head and make that three feet longer. So now you should be holding a concentration in which you can feel that your entire body is six feet longer than normal.

Next, return to the position of your elongated feet and create a long and expansive curved sweep to your right along the floor that runs from your feet in a wide semicircle to the new elongated position of your head. Once back at that point, rest. Then, create a wide sweep from your head along the floor to your left, again a semicircle that runs from your head to the new position of your feet. Once there, pause. Then run another semicircle high above you; again, begin at your feet, and curve all the way to your head. Then run a semicircle from your head down through the floor and back to your feet.

Now I want you to feel that your entire body is filling the circles you have created. Expand yourself north-south, east-west, above and below so that you are now massive in size. Hold that for a moment. Next, see yourself very small, about three inches in length. Imagine yourself lying on your own chest. Imagine that little person lying in the same direction as your body. Get inside that little person. Once inside, have that little person say your name three times. As he or she says your name, feel your identity inside that little body. To make the idea more real, have the little character wave one arm. Imagine yourself watching the arm on your chest. Decide how long the arm is. Then have the little person raise the other arm. Make that visualization alive. Have him or her smile and wriggle a little bit.

Next, go back to the expansive feeling, whereby you filled the entire circle with your presence. See if you can fill the entire circle with your mind. Once that is achieved, I want you very quickly to fold your energy inward, collapsing your thought-form from the expansive you into the little-you. Then breathe in slowly, and as you do see yourself expanding again, hold that at its outer expansion and then quickly collapse it back into the little person. Then breathe in slowly and expand again. Repeat this process half a dozen times.

By going from large to very small quickly, you begin to exercise the throat chakra; you may feel a tickling sensation there as the stiffness in the elasticity of the etheric web begins to change.

Next, have the little person get up from your chest and have it walk into your throat and disappear. Now visualize your body hovering about 18 inches above itself. Try to sustain that image strongly. You may feel the etheric rocking at this stage. Don't be alarmed. You are not going to fly off into never-never land. Just allow it to rock. It is a good sign. Next, you imagine yourself rolling like a log over to your right. See how far your roll will take you before your momentum ceases. Once out there, roll back so that you are hovering over your body once more. Then roll to your left and see how far that will go. Notice if there is a difference. Which roll went farther?

Now see yourself hovering over your body once more, and in your mind's eye, stand up. You now should be vertical at your feet. Hold that image for a moment. Then lean that character over to your right at an angle of 45 degrees. Hold that unusual position for a moment, then lean the character over to the left. Hold the same angle. Pause. Then lean it forward and away from you at a 45-degree angle, and then bring it back and have it lean backwards toward you at the same angle.

The leaning exercise helps the etheric web detach from its rigid position within your body. Now lean it back all the way so that it is over your physical body looking at the ceiling, and rotate it so that now you are face to face with your etheric self. Have it log roll once again.

Once done, bring it so that it hovers over you, facing you, and have it raise one hand and touch you on the cheek. See if you can feel that. Then have it repeat the process, touching you with the other hand on the other cheek.

Now have that image slide over your head, and once clear of your physical body, have it begin to rotate gently. If at this point it wants to fly off, let it. Follow it with your mind and notice everything. Especially notice if your feelings change. When that exercise is spent, bring it back and have it settle over your body. Then drop it gently inside of you once more. Take your concentration up to the top of your head, and now run around your body once more, delineating it with your concentration, and this time accentuate that concentration so that you feel that etheric around you, solid and powerful.

Now put your concentration into your right arm. Elongate that with your mind and hold that image for a moment. Then take a deep breath and really relax your body and see if you can drop your arm through the floor. Then try with your other arm. You may find that you can drop your whole body through, or perhaps just your legs. Attempt it anyway. About 25 percent manage to get through the floor with some part of their body on the first attempt. Others have to go at it longer. The etheric stretch is over. But lie there for a second to regain your composure. You may feel a little spacey and disoriented.

Perform the stretch at regular intervals. For a while, do it every day. Doing so, you enliven the etheric, and it allows you to sustain altered states of unusual perception without feeling uncomfortable. In the etheric, one deals with a dimension with which one is unfamiliar. This can cause panic. The level of discomfort depends also on your personality. If you are the kind of person who can move around the world easily, experiencing unusual situations without difficulty, then the etheric world becomes just another one of those experiences. If you are more regimented in your approach to life, then experiences that are outside your normal field of experience may cause your more concern.

Looking at the stretch, you can see how hard it is to follow the instructions by reading them and that a tape would be easier.

Second Etheric Move: The Spin

The Spin is like the stretch insomuch as it allows you to pull the etheric into new positions, thus enlivening it. Sit in an armchair with your back straight. If you have a theta metronome tape, use it for all your etheric exercises. You can use my *Art of Meditation* tape for this purpose. Body-talk yourself into a state of deep relaxation, then take your concentration to the top of your head and delineate your body at about a quarter of an inch, accentuating your energy with your concentration. As you go 'round your body with your mind, feel your presence in the physical plane. Feel yourself saying, *I am what I am. This is what I am, this is where I find myself. I accept that.*

Take your concentration to the top of your head and then visualize your personality or character stepping out of your body and standing in front of you at an angle of 45 degrees above you.

Put your feeling into where the heart of that character would be, standing as it is in front of you. Now lean that image away from you at an angle of 45 degrees. Hold that, then bring it back to the vertical position. Now lean it to the left at an angle of 45 degrees and hold that. Then again return to vertical. Now lean it to the right at an angle of 45 degrees and hold that, and then return to vertical. Finally, lean it back toward you at an angle of 45 degrees. Hold that for a moment, then return it to the normal upright position.

On completing these moves, return that image back to within your body and delineate your energy once more, starting at the crown and going all around your body. Now create the image once more, this time having it stand behind you, up and above you slightly at an angle of 45 degrees. Begin the leaning process, repeating the moves you just completed when the image was in front of you. Lean it back, then to the right, then to the left, and finally forward.

Once completed, return the image to within your body once more and outline your body strongly with your mind. Then rest for a moment. Create the image once more up and behind you, but this time accentuate your alignment to the visualization. Really feel that it is you. Hold that concentration about a minute, and then with the force of your will, have that image spin away in whatever direction is chooses. Notice everything while that spin is taking place.

After you have allowed that image to spin for a while, bring it back within the body and rest. Notice if you felt a sense of liberation and joy in the spin or not. Notice if you resisted the spin or if you cast yourself into it. Look and see if the energy of the spin was the same as your life or if it was in contrast, different.

Third Etheric Move: Stepping Out

These previous moves are practiced in meditation. This move, "stepping out," can be done either in meditation or at any time. It is a visualization in which you see yourself reversed inside your body, looking backwards. Imagine your etheric self turning, and while your body looks one way, your etheric identity faces the other. Once that image is held, have your etheric self walk out of your body in a straight line backwards. As it does so, you may feel a tugging sensation in the area of your solar plexus, or on occasion, you may feel one of your chakras reacting.

You can really help this exercise along if from time to time you just imagine what is behind you. It is like looking backwards with your mind, not with your sight. It opens you to the feeling that reality is not just in front of you, but all around.

The reversing process has a fascinating link to the spirit world. Often at the end of the tube, I found that reality there was reversed—like looking in a mirror. I thought about it for many months, and I received a lot of mirror imagery in my meditations. I knew that there was some link, but I was not sure what.

One day I was visiting with a friend, Sarah Estep, who is secretary of an organization called American Association of Electronic Voice Phenomena, which specializes in recording voices on tape from the spirit world. She told me that often the taped messages she records from the spirit world are recorded on the reverse of the tape going backwards. Electronically this is not logical. But I have listened to her tapes, and sure enough, many of the messages are on the wrong side of the tape and reversed.

Mrs. Estep told me that when she was just starting out recording the spirit voices, she had great difficulty. One day one of the communicators suggested that she place a mirror by the recording equipment. She did so, and the quality and quantity of recordings increased dramatically.

I have used the mirror in meditation to connect more strongly with the Higher Self, and I have also found it useful when working creatively, for it aligns one to one's intuition more strongly. I believe the mirror acts as a rudimentary satellite communicator. It allows you to focus on the inner worlds. The best mirrors are the concave type that are sold as shaving mirrors. Try it to see if it works for you.

The function of the etheric exercise is to manipulate the etheric, to loosen and enliven it. First, it will give you more energy, and second, it makes you less tight and more open to possibilities. By moving the Life Force, you begin to understand that it is an entity of itself, and that identity has abilities.

As the Life Force consolidates and strengthens, your ability to penetrate the inner worlds becomes possible. The keys are twofold. First, you have to train your mind to sustain deep levels of trance of the theta brain-wave type and not fall asleep. I don't want to take time in this book to explain how to do that. It is just a matter of practice. Get a theta metronome tape and practice every day. See how entranced you can become without dropping off. You are trying to get the brain down to about four or five cycles per second so that the electromagnetic field its oscillations create is lessened. When you get down low enough, the tube will appear. At first you may have difficulty traveling up the tube with your inner mind. Again, it takes practice. You have to "let go," and you have to have a concerted focus of will. I am going to discuss the turbo-thought effect in a later chapter. Suffice it to say that once your desire to get up the tube is strong enough and the focus is there, you go. Simple, really—it just takes time.

The second key is that in penetrating the etheric and the inner worlds, what one is saying basically is that one's evolution through the physical is more or less over. That does not mean you are going to die. It means you are demanding access to the next evolution while still a part of this one. To do so, one has to release the physical, going beyond any strong emotional attachment, and that, for many, is hard.

The *Quickening* is a process of etheric enlivenment, but the level on which one can accept that energy is directly linked with the level on which one is free from tick-tock. What the world believes metaphysically and spiritually is mostly drivel, and it holds the world back. To move up, you have to be prepared to let go and to stand on your own. Once you become a truly active participant in your own evolution, free from preconceived notions, able to travel upwards, you do. It's a lot of fun.

But first you have to obliterate tick-tock.

10

OBLITERATING
TICK-TOCK

To UNRAVEL tick-tock and set your spirit free, we first have to address the issue of the Quickening as it relates to the circle-people. Those of you who have read my other books, please play among yourselves for a moment while I explain the concept to those unfamiliar with it.

As was said earlier, we live inside a metaphysical circle or fence that is created by the electromagnetic oscillations of the brain. For generations, scientists have pondered the mysteries of the brain, only to be baffled by the fact that we seem to use but a small part of it. What is the function of the rest of the brain?

Interestingly enough, there are no parts of the body (except perhaps the appendix, which is a vestige of the old mammalian tail) that we don't use. Isn't it odd that the most important organ of the body seems for the most part redundant? Or is it? Could it be that the main function of the brain is its inhibition of the human? The brain and its oscillations act as an inhibitor, cutting one off from the perception of the inner worlds. It is only in death (when the brain stops) or in trance (when it slows down) that you become aware of another reality.

If your brain cells were not oscillating at speed, you would be open to a bombardment of information flowing in, not only from the inner worlds, but also from the thoughts of people around you. The mental cacophony would be overwhelming, and without the protection of the brain, you would be open to the eternal light shining constantly upon you. It would be impossible to concentrate on day-to-day life. Eventually, you would go mad with frustration. Life would seem an agonizing trap, and suicide would become commonplace. Inside the circle, it is impossible to come to a real understanding of the spiritual truth of things. So generation upon generation of circle-people have made up explanations as they go along, guessing for the most part what might exist beyond the circle. The mind of man is so easily influenced by anything that is expressed with conviction, by anyone in authority, that vast amounts of spiritual "twaddle" have been handed down for thousands of years, and the circle people, lacking alternatives, have needlessly encumbered their spirit and lapped it up.

The circle is dominated financially by the big families that own most of the world and by the institutions that the families have created to control the people. Spiritually, the circle is dominated by organized religions, which in the past were often tied financially to the big families. Those religions have dominated and controlled the people for a thousand years and more.

Socially and morally, the owners and organizers of the world have developed philosophies that disempower everyone, especially the ordinary people. This way each person can remain a pawn in the whole—giving his life and his efforts to support the whole. Because the environment of the circle-people is so totally controlled, it is impossible for them to experience life as it should be. Instead, they are forced to experience it through a system that denies them expression except in a most limited way. Even one's mind is programmed from early childhood to see things as it believes them to be. If one wore special lenses that, say, gave off a green hue, everything would look green for a while, but eventually the mind would adjust to the constant green hue, and it would turn the colors back to "natural" regardless of the color of light it was seeing through the lens. The mind adjusts to see whatever it believes. In the same way, your life adjusts to reflect and confirm exactly whatever you believe in.

Within the circle there are only limited possibilities. Meanwhile, the truth is always hidden from the circle-people so that what they think is happening is not usually all that is actually happening. The dominant institutions control the flow of information, and that information is tainted toward giving people a certain impression. Further, the information is presented in such a way as to give the impression that the institutions are independent, fair, and aboveboard. This in fact is not usually so; all the regulations are stacked against you. There are hardly any institutions that one does business with or which are a part of one's life that are not influenced or dominated behind the scenes by some vested interest.

Further, the ordinary man is kept so busy just making it through life that he has no time to check everything he is told. In fact, he is vehemently discouraged from developing an inquiring mind or an independent philosophy. Because the circle-people have no real way of checking the information they are given, they accept by habit whatever they are told.

For example, more than a million laws are imposed upon you. Yet have you ever read in the original form even one of those laws? How do you know that what the authorities say is the law is, in fact, the law? For example, millions of Americans file their tax returns on April 15 every year because they think that is the law of the land and that they are required to do so. It is not. Yet why do you think people follow along? Because the tax authorities have manipulated people into thinking that that is what is required. In fact, filing a tax return is voluntary, and when you do so you invalidate a number of your rights under the act. Now, is the IRS lying to the people? Sure it is. But how many Americans in tick-tock know that?

If you knew exactly what was going on and how deceived we are, you would go nuts. But you don't know—most likely you don't have time to care. And if you do care, there is nothing much you can do about it, so in the end you have to shrug and walk away. That is why the Warrior-Sage will not truck for one moment with the petty manipulations of mechanical-man—they are ungodly. The Force did not put us on this earth to be manipulated by faceless morons. There is no spiritual authority that says the Mickey Mouse institutions have power over you, none whatsoever. Yet that is the way it is. We have to accept that and work around it as best we can. If spirit-man wanted, he could influence millions, and he could even terrorize the institutions. For at their core, they are weak, and they rule over the halfhearted.

So why does spirit-man not dominate and control those in power for the betterment of mankind? Because the Warrior-Sage knows that to be king of a rabble is not a monarchy, it's a trap. Finally, when all was said and done and spirit-man tossed out all the manipulators, who then would run things? Eventually, one would have to hire more mechanical-men, and within a year or two the same nonsense would be reestablished and begin all over again.

So what is the answer? To walk away and let mechanical-man and his institutions control the people; for in the end, the controllers inherit only a bankrupt world: They dine on the bitter fruit of their manipulations. To escape to a *Quickening,* you have to realize that your only option is to walk. Sad in a way, yet it is the only option. In the end, all you can offer the world is your strength, your self-reliance, and your true freedom.

The circle-people live in a prison and are lulled into thinking they are free because they can choose between sausages and eggs for breakfast. They can't understand real freedom, partly because they are asleep and partly because there has never been a time when they were not in prison.

If one were born to a woman who was serving a life sentence and grew up in prison never having walked beyond its walls or seen the outside, one would get used to the restriction of prison life and eventually come to accept and actually enjoy it. Why do you think people live in a dump like Belfast or Moscow? The prison is safe. It becomes abhorrent for one to consider leaving. The jailer becomes a friend. As one grows older, one hears stories of people who lived outside the prison in the "heartland" of life, but one does not clearly understand the nature of their lives and the liberation and freedom the "heartlanders" seem to enjoy.

It's frightening. Most likely, one would criticize, making the heartlander's lifestyle "wrong" in prison terms, calling them "weirdos." The circle-people are the children born to the prisoner: Few escape. Some climb onto the walls and look out, but they don't actually leave. The few who do escape are rubbed from the memories of those who remain, by virtue of the fact that their energy is moving so much faster than that of those left behind. The heartlanders are labeled "renegades" by the circle-people.

Now you may say, "Well, I am free, so I must be beyond the walls of the prison." But are you? Delusion is a common trait in the circle. Each one tells the other that he is "special," more righteous than....or more chosen or selected than....and so forth. The competing egos of the children in the prison yard serve only to bind them ever so fiercely and to make the walls of their entrapment even more difficult to scale. Before the Warrior-Sage in the "heartland" would consider you free and a part of his or her world, you would have to successfully answer these questions:

What part of your mind is concerned with safety and survival, and how many of your daily thoughts center on these concerns?

How free are you to walk away from where you are now? What binds you emotionally? Can you release everything if you have to—family, friends, your neighborhoods, money, your country, your origins—everything you believe in?

What level of self-sustaining individuality have you mastered? Can you exist in a dimension of consciousness where there is no one to help you, to save you if you fall, to advise you? Can you walk through life unassisted?

What measure of loneliness can you sustain?

What depth of "trust" lies within you? Can you place your fate in an invisible world, where no one recognizes you or thanks you if you do well, where there is no ego gratification, no awards, no accolades?

Is the belief that you have in yourself and your individuality unassailable? Can you back yourself forever, right or wrong, through thick and thin, regardless of circumstances? Or is your belief vulnerable? Would the Warrior-Sage be able to walk up to your weak spot and rattle your insecurities, forcing you to run?

What do you feel about the world of the circle-people? Can you leave it alone? Can you allow them their destiny, changing nothing? Is there anything the circle-people could do or say to you that would upset you or influence your decisions? Do you act to keep people happy? Do you, through weakness, seek their approval? Is this your method to try to win people over? If so, why? If you are settled inside yourself, you don't have to win people's affections. They either like you or they don't. Their opinion is irrelevant.

What of the institutions? Do you believe in them, or can you see them for what they are?

Money—do you absolutely control your needs, or are you reliant on others? Do you dominate your destiny, or are you affirming your prison sentence by paying into the pension plan? Are you creating your own obsolescence, trotting mechanically toward your retirement? Warrior-Sages never quit, never retire, never finish, never rest.

What of your philosophy of life? Is it yours? Have you proven it to yourself? What questions have you asked? Or are you blindly following some "twaddle" you read about? What does it mean to you? What part is anger, manipulation, holier-than-thou? What part calls on you to serve, and for what cause? What part is a mechanical-man's survival trip? What part sets you free; what binds? Could you bag it all and start again, realizing that it served you but that its function was not necessarily permanent?

Finally, what of the *Quickening?* Is it just a few gummy spiritual platitudes, standing in the light and all that good stuff, channeled perhaps from the armpit of some "spaco," or does it frighten you? If it does not, you may not even be close.

If you can answer all or most of these questions correctly and powerfully, you are on the wall at the very least. Jump! The grappling hooks of mechanical-man will always try to get you back. Once on the wall you may rest awhile, but sooner or later, you commit to the "heartland" or you fall. You have talked of your power. "Now show me," challenges the Warrior-Sage.

At this point, you are either nauseated by this whole *Quickening* philosophy and thinking, *I'll trash this book—better still, I'll mail it to someone I don't like*—or you are thinking, *It's true, I know it's true. There's a freedom, an exhilaration, a special world—maybe this Bozo knows what he's talkin' about after all. How do I join? What do I need to do?*

The first trick is to learn to stay awake in a world where everyone is asleep for the most part—lulled into a somnolence by the oscillation of the brain on the one hand and the oscillation of the electromagnetic field of the earth on the other. The earth vibrates at seven hertz-per-second, which, of course, is the same speed as the alpha brainwave or dream state.

As I've said, learning to stay awake means forcing the mind to pay attention and to concentrate on life. A simple concept but hard to do. It involves pulling your energy within yourself and concentrating only on those things that are important to you. It involves doing things constantly that will discipline you to stay awake. More than anything else, staying awake means becoming enthusiastically committed to yourself. How excited are you by what you are? You have to back yourself, otherwise who will?

In a world where people hate responsibility, avoid commitment, and shun reality, what you are looking to do is the very opposite. You are creating through your commitment to your quest, through your enthusiasm for truth, an affirmation that says: "I'll step up. I'll take control. I accept what I am, and I commit totally and absolutely to my life. Not one second of it will I waste in the nonsense of mechanical-man. I am what I am, and what I am is getting stronger and more independent each day. I might have been a bit wimpy in the past, but I'm becoming strong, crafty, and quick."

Then, as you walk toward a new world, a new brotherhood, you will allow yourself, through self-acceptance, the time needed to make the kind of changes you want. In the same way that you are not going to mess with trying to impress the world or trying to accommodate it, so too you will not try to accommodate what your ego thinks you should do. What does it know anyway? Its religion is fear and insecurity. You will set your path through commitment, you will be happy in "not knowing," and you will walk. You will not listen to the demands of the ego that says that life has to be guaranteed, cozy, and safe. Instead, you will deliberately design a life that is not necessarily any of these, a life that endorses you, a life of experience and excitement, a life that is truly lived.

There is a point that you will reach, if you haven't gotten

there already, where the resonance of mechanical-man will drive you mad. You will see the tick-tock in your life, and you will wake to its utter uselessness, its crushing boredom. You will not be able to take it a moment longer. Tick-tock becomes a symbol of your weakness, and in the end, you have to walk away or stay in the frustration of knowing that you are in prison, that the doors are open and you lack the courage to walk out.

I can forgive myself anything except being boring. And it's true that we bore ourselves silly—trotting as we do back and forth over the same ground doing the same dumb things ad infinitum, until one day we realize the futility of it all. We are shocked to discover that we suffer from metaphysical body odor—owners of a hundred hackneyed concepts that we haven't washed or changed in years, concepts that were fresh when we donned them but that are now putrid because, in our silliness, we made them permanent. We created dogma because it was easier than inventing new ideas.

Either the *Quickening* will bump you and you'll never get out, or you will dump tick-tock and jump. I would rather cast my fate to the unknown than bore myself to death anytime.

I was in Melbourne, Australia, recently, giving a lecture in a hotel on the subject of staying awake. During the break, I popped downstairs to get a pack of gum. Journeying back to the main ballroom, I was waiting in the hallway for the elevator when I noticed two gentlemen from the Orient, obviously business executives. Now in recounting this story I don't mean to imply that folk from the Orient are more asleep than others, for generally speaking they are not, but these two characters had pillows surgically stitched to their ears!

The elevator door opened and I walked in. Meanwhile, Yamamoto and Toshiba in the hallway went through incredible gyrations trying to decide if they wanted to use the elevator or not. They bounced back and forth, bobbing and bowing like marionettes on a music box. Finally, the elevator door began to close. Whereupon Yamamoto, who was obviously the junior of the two, made a kamikaze plunge for the elevator.

The hotel in Melbourne was fairly old. Nowadays in modern hotels, if the elevator begins to shut, all you do is touch the rubber strip in the door and it bounces back. Unfortunately, the rubber-strip technology must have been unavailable in Melbourne in the olden days, for once the elevator door decided to close, there was nothing anyone could do about it. Yamamoto got his head firmly stuck in the door!

Frantically, I tried to pry the door open from within, to no avail. Now if you have traveled around a bit, you will know that no two elevators anywhere in the world have the same button configuration. There are a hundred possible selections. There is M for Mezzanine, G for Ground, L for Lobby, the LL for the Lower Lobby, #1 for the first floor—except if you are in Britain, where #1 is for the second floor—and so on. I scanned the console looking for the button marked "Release Oriental Gent" and found none. Meanwhile, Yamamoto was going through a major loss of face, and I could not help wondering what he looked like from his boss's view back in the hallway.

Anyway, to make a long story short, I finally got him unstuck, and he retreated back to his boss, who no doubt by now had canceled his promotion for being silly. Of course, here in the West we don't understand how bad a loss of face can be to an Oriental. It is not a major concern of ours; we are more worried about losing our hubcaps! But to Yamamoto, the elevator incident was hell on high water.

Anyway, that little bit of "life's rich tapestry" served to remind me that most of the world is asleep and that, as part of the *Quickening,* we have to remember to stay awake. You might try thumping yourself on the nose every so often if you start to falter.

If one were to plot a graph through the consciousness of tick-tock, taking the most restricted person in the world—the one with the tightest feelings—and giving him a factor of "struggle #1," then taking the next most restricted person and giving him a factor of "struggle #2," and so forth, one would find people of similar levels of consciousness standing around each other. This is true metaphysically and geographically. Through correspondence, people are pulled to communities and areas that reflect what they feel: The neighborhood becomes a symbol of what they are. People of similar mental attitudes, although they be from various philosophies and backgrounds, reenact the common restrictions the world over.

Even though those restrictions are expressed in different languages and cultures, they are aspects of the same binding. Thus, a Catholic peasant in southern Sicily has the same psychological disabilities as does a Moslem in Tangier or a Buddhist rice farmer in the East. They each possess the same fatalism. They all believe in the overpowering presence of chance, and they feel unable to dominate their own lives.

As we plot the graph to include those who are more free, the lines would open up, and in the end, the theoretical diagram would look like the conical shape of the spirit world, but expressed here on earth as a measure of the consciousness of the people.

We can see that those who have rediscovered their true identity stand a long way from those in the center or funnel of the cone, and that the cone itself traps those found toward the bottom of it. As one becomes more free and independent, one begins to climb out of the funnel, moving along a curved parabola toward the outside of the circle.

In the bottom of the cone, one's ability to move is so restricted that one can't really conceive of the possibility. Because the horizon is limited, all that can be seen are others in similar circumstances gathered nearby. They serve to confirm that life is indeed the restriction and struggle one believes it to be. So naturally one is forced, through limited vision or a lack of social opportunity, to concentrate on that restriction.

In the lower end of tick-tock, people develop interpersonal relationships. They live in closely knit tribal communities, and the family unit is usually large and also closely knit. The overriding concern of the people is the circumstance of life, its terms and conditions, so to speak. They perceive danger and negativity all around them, and that forces them to concentrate on survival, on saving each other. Each holds on to the other in a state of helplessness.

As one climbs out of the tighter area of the cone into where the parabola curves, the restriction is much less, and the power flowing from the inner worlds becomes greater. This is not because there is nay high or low or because God likes free people more than he likes tight ones, but because as one becomes more free, one also becomes less fearful, and the etheric web opens up to allow more energy into one's life. It is as if by moving toward freedom one is granted additional power that assists in the search for that freedom.

Once out of the funnel, one reaches an area of greater metaphysical possibilities, and the horizon is no longer restricted. One's vision becomes limitless, and although one may feel a little lost because life is less structured, one intuits that that new power is now available, and that is exciting. As one continues to climb, it is apparent that there is an edge to the circle, and there may be a vague sense of knowing that beyond the circle lies an incredible world. It is doubtful that at this stage one would know what that world means, but it can definitely be identified as the source of light.

The light intensifies as one begins to concentrate on it. By now, its power is greater than the emotional ups and downs of life, and as one identifies with it in simple, uncluttered terms, it begins to pull toward itself. So now one's journey is no longer empowered just by personal effort; there is also a Force, a current. One proceeds toward it in constant motion even though one may not be intellectually aware of that progress.

Presently, the concerns of those trapped in the cone are no longer a part of one's consciousness. Their negative influence is no longer a factor, and their restrictive lifestyles no longer offer a negative proof of one's own life. People may say this attitude is callous, but it comes from a true dedication to the quest, and as one proceeds, one distances oneself naturally from the concerns of the circle-people. To concentrate on one's quest is not callous once one understands the importance of it and the position in which one finds oneself. It may be callous for a person in the deeper part of the funnel to ignore the misery of others, for by his very position in the cone he has a responsibility for them, but for another farther away, this alignment vanishes. In fact, the situation of the people in the funnel becomes a symbol of everything one has left behind, so it is unattractive. One turns instead to a dedication to higher things.

One can understand how in their circumstances most people do not see their lives as necessarily restricted. That is because their horizon is limited by those standing around them, so they only experience the ideas of others. As concepts are repeated over and over, they solidify into truth, and eventually it seems to those in the funnel that all humanity is in the same circumstances they are. They become resigned to their fate, perhaps feeling that there might be more, but they look around and see that there is no more and so continue living just through that.

As a Warrior-Sage, one may wish that everyone could begin to climb to a new level, but that is not going to happen just yet, and one has to be careful not to waste energy yearning for something we don't have. The same inner light is available to those in the funnel, the difference being that the Warrior-Sage is more open to receive it and that it comes from a place that is "across" from rather than "above." So the God-Force is not a controlling influence from above, rather an ally of which one is a part. It is the restriction in the funnel that creates the psychological illusion that the God-Force is above. The impression is of looking up. Once on the curve, one is looking across.

Looking back down the funnel of the cone, one can see that at the bottom are the world's poor, those whose economic circumstances and beliefs usually affirm their restriction. Then coming up the funnel, the sides of which are no less steep, are the richer people—those who, though their outlook is still restricted by the cone, are in a position to feel more self-worth because mechanical-man sees money as a symbol of that self-worth. In addition, those of better economic circumstances are more likely to travel, and so become less stiff by being exposed to a wider set of circumstances.

They have the chance to climb if they can turn away from all that they believe to be true and can cast away the tribal binding. I am not talking about millionaires, but about those who have a reasonably comfortable lifestyle in which most of their needs are met. This allows them to move beyond the more intense, mechanical-man struggle to survive, and they can begin to look around for other possibilities.

That is why men who normally do not possess a natural spirituality do not often look at their lives in spiritual terms until they have succeeded economically. It is almost as if the male has to burn out himself and his ego in the marketplaces of life in order to see himself in a good light. Then and only then can he begin to look up and out of the cone toward his real spirituality, toward the Warrior-Sage and an independent philosophy.

The female generally takes on the restriction of the inner core in a more spatial and less intellectual way than does the male. He will be rigorously involved in sustaining the dogma. Since he sees it intellectually, he logically adopts an attitude that says that if he follows these rules exactly and precisely, if he supports and sustains this philosophy, then he will become "special" in the eye of God, and that will make him feel better. The female, however, possessing as she does a more natural spirituality, is less concerned with feeling okay. She knows she's okay. Her concern is not one of ego trying to be "special." Rather, she deals with feeling secure inside a mechanical-man survival mode, from a position that on the surface looks less physically strong than the male's.

Her position within the philosophy is of nurturer, not sustainer. Her attitude is usually more free and more lovingly accepting of others. Though she may not have the personal security or power necessary to toss out the philosophy, she will take it to her heart in a less dogmatic way, using it to further the goodness or the nurturing, and adapting it somewhat to fit her feelings.

11

SPIRITUAL CONCEPTS YOU'LL PROBABLY NEVER NEED

WHEN YOU look at the philosophies that have been adopted by the masses, you can see that they are deliberately designed to keep the people asleep. That is why in Moslem or Christian services, one does not engage in lively debate of the issues. One repeats over and over again the same chants or prayers, thus programming the mind to accept without question whatever is offered.

The philosophies serve as "glue" to hold the tribes together in a psychic bonding. In fact, the word *religion* comes from the Latin word *religare*, which means "to bind." The overall function of these philosophies is to assist those of like mind to process emotion and fear in what are basically the difficult circumstances of their lives. The psychic bonding makes it almost impossible for a person to develop a true individuality, for the most important part of him, his spiritual alignment, is regimented and structured and often laced with regulations covering every aspect of his behavior. This forces him either to follow along like a good sheep or to infringe on those laws, suffering as he will all the inherent recriminations and guilt. Heads you lose, tails you can't win.

It amazes me, with all the technological advances we have made, how it is that we have not upgraded our philosophies. There is no shortage of great thinkers, yet somehow our spiritual approach to God hasn't progressed much over the ages.

I am not sure how many people I have met in my travels— many hundreds of thousands I would imagine. Yet after two million miles and fifty countries, I don't think I have encountered more than a couple of hundred people whom I would consider of the Warrior-Sage class. Beyond these, there have been perhaps a couple of thousand who had the makings of true power yet had some way to go. The rest were lovely but wimpy.

One thing I know is that I met few who were a part of an institutional religious philosophy and who had any real power to speak of. There have been some exceptions, but generally this was the case. Because the God-Force is spontaneous and liberating, it seems impossible to really get in touch with your spirituality until you can wander off philosophically and discover yourself. As for the energy of the Warrior-Sage, it is almost impossible to develop that in the company of others.

Does this mean that all of the religions are useless? I don't think so. They perform a function and grant to mechanical-man a morality without which our societies would become impossible to control. In addition, within, say, Christianity, there are many factions—60,000, approximately. Some of them hold on to their flock with a vicelike grip. Others are more liberal.

I have lectured in many New Thought Christian churches such as Unity and those Science of Mind churches centered around the philosophy of Ernest Holmes. What makes these organizations so refreshingly different is that they are based on helping the individual to become free, not on controlling him or her. They teach affirmations and abundance, and they show an individual how to make the most of his or her life. I have never once heard a minister from one of these churches talk about sin or guilt. Ironically, Unity and Science of Mind are very successful, especially in the United States. So it proves that one can create a church that does not manipulate or control the congregation and can still make it financially. In contrast, if you look at many of the other Christian movements, you can see that they are based on emotion and various forms of negative manipulation. If Jesus shows up, as these churches teach, he'll throw up when he sees that lot. To use fear, negativity, guilt, and other forms of emotional pressure is a natural part of the experience of tick-tock. People expect it; it's part of their destiny at that level. But that does not excuse it, in my view.

The emotional hocus-pocus played by these churches on the individual actually helps some of the congregation in the end, for as the manipulations are laid on thick and fast, it forces those members who are destined to climb out to begin to reevaluate their lives and make their moves. For example, in the Catholic Church there is a group of laws that strictly regulate sexuality. What a group of all-male celibate priests would know about sexuality is beyond me, but anyway, these laws infringe upon the people who ought to be able to decide for themselves what is appropriate and loving and what is not.

One of the main bones of contention deals with contraception. The church's view is that Catholics should crank out "chubbies" (kids) willy-nilly so that the church gets more members. The individual parishioners don't generally agree with that because they are the ones who have to feed, clothe, and raise the children. For many Catholics, the contraception issue was the last straw, and they left the Church. In fact, the Catholic Church is going backwards in all modern societies; people are leaving in droves. The only place it makes some headway is in the Third World, where the citizens have not as yet developed the sophistication to question the Church's rulings.

You can imagine how hard it is for a person who is raised a Catholic to walk away from his church and to live with the thought that, if the church is right, when he gets to the Pearly Gates, Jesus will be there wagging his finger, and that individual will be cast into hell for all eternity. That's heavy. You need a lot of individuality, strength, and personal charisma to walk away from a manipulation that intense. Of course it is a load of baloney, and of all the experiences I have personally had in the presence of the light, I have never felt for one moment that there was any judgment about or comment on my actions. Rather, it reflected back to me aspects of myself, so I learned. Further, nothing about the God-Force gave me any impression that it was Catholic or even Christian. Unconditional love has to include unconditional acceptance and forgiveness. To create a judgmental God and sell that to the people as fact is an outright lie. But many believe it, and they accept without question the emotional "whammy" put on them.

Thus, the philosophies become self-policing. No one is awake enough to ask any awkward questions. People existing as they do in the bottom of the cone, the energy of which serves to keep the masses bound, have to either blindly accept like blithering idiots and trot along with the "great unwashed" or begin to ask awkward questions.

For example, in the Koran it says (loosely translated) that if you are having trouble with your wife, you should pop into the tent and punch her in the mouth. Now millions of Moslems accept the Koran as written instructions from God. Yet if I were Muslim, that sentence alone would stimulate my concern as to where God was the day he delivered that idea.

Muhammad, the prophet of God, could not read or write. Yet

somehow he sat in a cave and channeled all this good stuff that God wanted him to put down, and a billion people follow along. You can just imagine the scene. Muhammad is sitting in his cave troubled by the relationship with his wife. So he calls upon God to give him a little guidance, saying, "Excuse me, God, what do I do about my missus?"

God, who was taking a couple of days off from running the Universe, decides to handle Muhammad's inquiry. Now you may expect God to suggest that the Prophet talk to his wife and relate to her in a loving way and come to some reasonable compromise. But no. God says to the Prophet, "Remember this: If your ol' lady gives you trouble, pop in the tent and give her a right thump in the ear. Then tell that to your mates, so that 500 million Muslim women can live as second-class citizens for 1,500 years. That should work just fine."

Now you may be excused for thinking perhaps God was hittin' the gin that week, or perhaps everyone got a little confused. But you are bound to ask: How come he did not offer us a number of alternatives as well?

I am sure Muhammad's relationship with his God was an honorable one. But we have the right to ask questions if only to try to understand what is being said. In contrast, mechanical-man accepts philosophies as fact and goes back to concentrating on survival. Even the intelligentsia of mechanical-man stays within the intellectual tracks laid down, never moving into critical thinking, which asks so many unanswerable questions. It is not the function of mechanical-man to question, for if he does, he threatens the emotional and psychic safety of the others. So questioning the very essence of much of the "twaddle" that is offered as the word of God is taboo.

But if you are a bit of a metaphysical scamp, you can have a marvelous time looking at things, wondering why people are so thick, believing the stuff they do. For example, if you knew nothing about Christianity and you had never heard of the Bible, you would pick up the book and ask the critical question, "Who wrote this stuff?" "Er...well, actually no one knows. But it's the sacred, channeled word of God." "Fine," you'd say, "I can possibly use a little of that," and you'd read on.

In the first few pages of Genesis, you would notice that it says, in chapter 1, verse 27, that God created man and woman on the sixth day. "Fine, no problem." But a page later, in chapter 2, you would read that God did not make man and woman on the sixth day. In fact, the writer claims that God made Adam first. Then God stuck Adam in the garden of Eden, but that didn't work too well, as Adam got sick of living on his own in a botanical zoo. So God put Adam into a deep sleep and fashioned Eve from his rib. Now at this point you might wonder what the hell's going on. Perhaps, you might ask, Who is this space cadet who's doing all this good stuff? Anyway, after plowing laboriously through the Old Testament with all its violence and mayhem, you might justifiably come to the conclusion that the Old Testament is just the story of a bunch of Jewish hippies who were none too together.

How would you come to that conclusion? Well, you would read that it took them 40 years to make it from Egypt to the Promised Land (a distance of about 250 miles). You would conclude that they must have been as thick as two bricks or hardly nailed down. It wouldn't take a genius to work out that these characters, God's guided ones, proceeded at the heady pace of 30 yards a day, or 45 inches an hour! Any physically fit ant could have beaten this bunch to the Promised Land by about 30 years! If you think about it, it is very hard to walk at that pace—one's leg is constantly dangling in the air! I suppose it might have been a form of Biblical tai chi, but if you were "chosen" and guided by the hand of God, you might be excused for expecting a slightly better forward progress. A decent running back in the NFL can make a hundred yards in an hour with everyone trying to stop him. "I wonder who was tackling the Jews?" you'd ask.

Of course, the popular explanation is that God was stalling the Jews while they became worthy. The idea that the God-Force, the supreme and magnanimous energy in the vastness of all things, is dishing out little bits of real estate to one tribe over another is pure tick-tock. It is much more likely that the lads invented the Promised Land routine to justify knocking off someone else's territory. But I don't have a problem with that. In those days, pinching other people's land was common practice, and it was not considered immoral. Anyway, somewhere along this ludicrous story, God got thoroughly fed up with this bunch, so he called their leader Big Mo' up on a hill to give him a new game plan. Picture the scene: God's watching the Jews bumping into each other heading off in the wrong direction in all manner of confusion, so he decides to write down ten rules that he feels might help. Then he calls on Big Mo' to meet him in a secluded spot where God gives Big Mo' a couple of gold tablets.

Now here's the question: What form did God take on the mountain? He could not have been just a wispy angel, for those tablets must have been fairly heavy. He would have to have had at least a 30-pound grip, otherwise Big Mo' would have wound up with the tablets on his toe. So if God was not an angel, he must have turned himself into a man for Big Mo's benefit. Now think of Big Mo's view. He's puffing and wheezing up this bloody mountain, and there is this geezer holding two tablets. The fellow tells Big Mo' that he is God and that Big Mo' should haul these tablets back to the lads in the valley to help them on a bit.

Interestingly, Big Mo' doesn't bother to ask the fellow for ID nor does he read the tablets, for if he had he would have discovered that there wasn't a positive, liberating thought contained on them anywhere. The tablets were a list of do's and don'ts, and by now Big Mo's wondering why the hell God couldn't just give him a map with an arrow on it saying: Promised Land This Way.

Anyway, Big Mo' doesn't ask questions such as: I wonder where God got the gold from? Instead he heads back to camp, where it seems the lads have gotten a little out of control, and all manner of tomfoolery is going on. Big Mo' is "pooped" from hauling all this stuff up and down the bloody mountain, and naturally the fellow is a little frazzled and in no mood for a party. He sees the lads cavorting about having a great time, and Big Mo' gets really pissed off and starts punching out the team mascot, a golden calf. To make a long story short, no one knows if God's game plan actually helped the Jews find the Promised Land, but history recounts that eventually, by process of elimination, they made it.

I must say, if I had been hanging around for 40 years and God finally gave me a lump of rock like Israel, I would be a little bit disappointed. To me, Promised Land would be the South of France, California, or the Cotswolds in the West of England. But perhaps the lads were too tired to notice that God had dealt them a bum rap.

Anyway, reading on, we find that from these high-stepping pioneers came Jesus of Nazareth, the Son of God. J. C.'s mum was married to an ol' guy called Joe who, it seems was a bit past it. God himself wasn't up for the task either, so he sent one of his mates, Gabe, for a little "coitus celestius." Nine months later, Jesus was born in a low-cost housing project in Bethlehem.

Now we know that he wasn't the Son of God because the Big Guy sent his mate Gabe. Perhaps he wasn't even the son of Gabe, for no one knows for sure whether Gabe and J. C.'s mum ever got it together. Perhaps ol' Joe made a miraculous comeback. Anyway, we can overlook all that stuff, because any hope of making sense of the story was lost some time back with Mo' on the playing fields of the Promised Land.

Now we turn to the nitty-gritty, the Gospels. Again, we are not allowed to ask who wrote them. We are expected to accept the author's veracity blindly and to refer to the authors via their pen names: Matthew, Mark, Luke, and John. Again these works are supposedly the channeled revelations of God. Read on, Boo-boo, this is the real stuff.

The first thing our metaphysical scamp notices is that God must have been fairly illiterate, for the Gospels are poorly written: they jump around a lot and are packed with inconsistencies. Disappointed, our scamp puts the book down for a moment and muses about why there are four Gospels?

If it was so important for God to channel the story correctly, why then did he repeat himself four times, and why are the stories so totally different, each contradicting the others? None of the Gospels agree as to what happened. And it seems that none of the Gospelers ever met Jesus: The Gospels were all written at different times. One would have to presume that either God had an incredibly poor memory, or he had some kind of cosmic twitch whereby every decade or so he would sit bolt upright, and, for no explicable reason, blurt out the story he had told years back, forgetting what he said last time.

In the end, you are left with two alternatives: Either God is a complete nitwit, or the Gospels are not the sacred, channeled words of God after all; but are rather a collection of writings from the same space cadets who were running 40-year tours to the Promised Land.

Now if you look at what is being offered in the New Age as the channeled word of God, you can see that not much has changed in 2,000 years. Many of the writers are spacey and full of their own spiritual self-importance, and people lap it up. Is it any surprise that the Gospels worked so well as a promo? People love that stuff. It takes them out of day-to-day living, and that is why nowadays there is a channeler on every corner. In fact, there are so many channels that sooner or later God will have to go cable.

I recently heard of a fairly well-known New Age character who is claiming that she is having a virgin birth. As I pen these words, she is about three months away from delivering another Messiah. That Gabe must have been lurking about again.

Of course in tick-tock, no one is allowed to question the truth of all this stuff. If you do, you will be labeled the anti-Christ—or anti-Jewish or anti-Buddhist or whatever—for even suggesting that much of this is a bunch of hogwash.

But our metaphysical scamp means no harm: He is just thinking aloud. There is no way that he would ever dream of changing anything, for he or she respects things as they are and realizes that in tick-tock, things are supposed to stay that way. The people will leave once they have sufficient strength, and not before.

The institutions control tick-tock by discouraging awkward questions. A bit like Russia, really. If you don't agree with the Communist Party, they throw you in a psychiatric hospital and call you mad. But our metaphysical scamp is not anti-anything. He is just pro the individual and pro a sensible approach.

The God-Force is energy. That energy has no volition of its own. It is not involved in what goes on. It makes no rules, and contrary to the assertions of all the major religions, it does not watch the individual acts of people, judge them, or create their reality for them. To say an event is the will of Allah is to say I haven't a clue how it came about. If one looks into the event and looks at what went on, one will see that those involved in the event created it solely through their energy—nothing else.

But one has to be fairly metaphysically sophisticated to accept a philosophy like that, because it leaves one out on one's own with no one to blame when things go wrong. It's natural for the Warrior-Sage to take responsibility for himself and his life. It is not natural in tick-tock, for within it no one really conceives of the idea that they might be able to do so; that is why they create little stories instead.

Once you can simplify your spiritual approach and bag the clutter, your energy begins to move faster, and the *Quickening* becomes a possibility. First, because you wind up with fewer obligations to God. (You have none really; you are God.) Second, the psychic binding of the philosophies is loosened.

It is more or less impossible to reach a point of true power inside the twaddle of tick-tock, so in order to create the *Quickening,* you will have to think in terms of liberating your spirit and allowing it to run free for a while. How about a three-year period when you have no philosophy at all; you just experience life and enjoy it and learn about yourself? Then, perhaps, once you have taken a sabbatical from tick-tock, you could create your own philosophy—one that honors and nurtures you, one that is designed to make *you* strong, not everyone else.

12

ACCELERATING THE QUICKENING

B ECAUSE THE overriding emotion of mechanical-man is survival, it is important for him to know what is going on at all
times. That is why fortune-tellers have always prospered. They
appeal to mechanical-man's need to know that all will be well.
Mechanical-man cannot rest where he finds himself. He has to
project into the future, asking what will happen. Will I be safe?
Will I be okay? Even if things are fine right now, he worries that
perhaps in the future things may fall apart and he won't make it.

The Warrior-Sage, because he is detached from concerns
about his death, is also not concerned about the future. He has no
need to know. He feels his energy powerfully and knows that
when the time comes, that same energy will affect his destiny,
creating strong circumstances as it does today. Knowing that to
be fact, the Warrior-Sage is not involved in having to know. He is
happy to settle in the present, and he realizes that in not knowing,

there is a power.

Only fools yearn to know. Their yearning becomes an affirmation of their weakness, for in that yearning, they affirm that they are insecure about sustaining a level of power that will deliver to them all that they need. By not having to know, one quickens and consolidates energy, for little of one's consciousness is in future-thought, and none in one's emotions. The great riddles of the universe remain, for the most part, unsolved. To chase after them seems to me a worthless endeavor. If we were supposed to know all the answers, we would have been given them.

Now one may ask, "How does one visualize and affirm a better future without drifting into future-thought?" The key is emotion. One can set up a battle plan, or goal, that one is aiming for, but if one's emotions are in play, then it will become an affirmation of lack. The best way to set up the goal is to know it to be granted and to be happy if it does not come about exactly the way one imagined.

It is obvious that we have to discover ourselves when we don't have all the facts by settling into an attitude of not-knowing to calm the spirit. Whatever reality presents itself is whatever one has created. Once a person can accept that, he or she begins to live within a personal energy level rather than within a mental-emotional projection. By accentuating what one is, one's energy becomes more powerful, and all those parts that one is *not* fall away, since they are no longer being sustained with one's emotions.

What defines reality as we understand it is the physical presence of an object—its height, breadth, and width, say. The object also is defined by where it isn't. In other words, it's the space around reality that grants to reality its validity. When one looks at a tree, one sees the branches and leaves. Yet what defines the tree are all those places where there are no branches or leaves. So as one concentrates on, say, the sky around the tree, it is the place where the tree is not that allows one to define precisely where the tree is. If the tree were so massive that it encompassed the whole scene and obliterated the sky, one could not correctly define its ramifications. One would have no clear idea of where the tree was and of where it was not.

Similarly, within the physical plane, there is a place where the body is, and there is a large area where it is not. Now you may never have thought in terms of what you are not, or of where you are not, or even of who you are not, but those contrary aspects are vital to you as you approach the non-world, or the etheric.

Let us look at how the concept of the non-being affects the power of one's thoughts. Because mechanical-man is not comfortable with himself, he has difficulty accepting things as they are. His consciousness is frequently some place other than where he finds himself.

Imagine him standing in a bubble of energy that contains all that he is, and imagine him constantly projecting wispy trails of consciousness away from him. Those wispy trails usually contain various aspects of his uncertainty about life. They are like streamers that flow in the wind of his consciousness. First, they contain emotional and mental energies that rob him of his power. Second, they create an aura around him that is ill defined.

Mechanical-man's future thoughts, his negative yearnings, and constant confusion flow from his consciousness to occupy, momentarily, a part of that space where he is not. Imagine a tree that is giving off large amounts of steam. The definition of the tree, where it is and where it is not, would become clouded by the stream. Mechanical-man's consciousness is like steam; it clouds him. The boundary of what he is and what he is not becomes confused. Thus, the consolidation that he seeks eludes him. By pulling your mind back from all those thoughts that take you into areas where you are not, you allow your etheric energy—the Life Force—to consolidate. What you are concentrates around you and becomes more powerful.

Future-thought is as irrelevant as yearning for the past. Of course one can recall a past event, especially if one wants to review the lessons learned from it. But yearning for the good ol' days is a dissipation of energy. First, the thought carries within it emotional energy. Second, the yearning becomes an affirmation that life now is not okay and that perhaps one has no ability to recapture the old grandeur. This, of course, is not true.

The power of the Warrior-Sage comes from his internalizing reality. This is more than the cliche of "owning one's own life." It is the process whereby one absolutely knows that one has created one's own reality and one stands alone and accepts that reality. It is easy to say, "I create my own reality," and then when things go wrong, to allow oneself to be emotionally imbalanced by whatever one is experiencing. By incarnating into a physical body, we automatically leave ourselves open to the ups and downs of life. The Warrior-Sage accepts that without comment, internalizing his experiences and making the most of them.

If, say, one finds oneself walking in mud up to the ankles, rain pouring on one's head, icicles trickling down one's neck, it is easy to complain or to blame someone else. "It's Harry's fault, he didn't come to pick me up, and now I am wet and miserable."

The Warrior-Sage would accept his wet condition as a part of life's possibilities and would make no comment. He accepts his discomfort and realizes that it is part of the glory of humanhood; it is his. He may, in passing, reflect on why he pulled these circumstances to himself, and he would conclude that sometimes it rains. Mostly he would get into the idea of being soaking wet— acting it out, living it to the full. The value he would receive is that he would have an opportunity to train his feelings. Here is a chance to feel powerful, consolidated, and happy even though he is soaked. He knows that the universe does not consider his wetness a misfortune, so neither will he. The rain is not aware of the discomfort it causes. He, too, is not emotionally aware. The Warrior-Sage lives circumstances to the fullest in order to get more out of the comfort of a warm fire he finds himself beside, by virtue of the fact that he was able to stay conscious and awake when he was not comfortable.

If one goes into a lousy restaurant and the food is revolting, one could complain to the management. However, that usually gets you nowhere, for on an inner level they know the place is lousy, and they like it that way. They cater only to people who need the "lousy restaurant" experience. For one to moan that there is a cockroach running around the coffee cup only confirms to them how well they are doing. While chewing through the revolting meal, one can remember every mouthful so that the next time one's faced with delicious foods, one won't chomp them down in a mechanical, tick-tock way. One will remember to enjoy them. Every time one acknowledges the reverse—the non-being—one claims reality as one's own. With each view there is an opposite. Tick-tock shows us the one direction; non-being shows us the other.

I was walking on a street in New York with some very holy-moly folk. They were top nobs in the New Age, very nice people, but boring in their righteousness. They carried with them a full accouterment of New Age symbols: the Indian skirt with the miso stain, Shakti sandals, the whole nine yards. We were talking about abundance and the New Age. As we chatted, a beggar came up to me and rattled his tin cup under my nose. I took 25 cents and thanked him. The beggar, having been flipped into a reverse, was stunned. The holy-molies unraveled—from the miso stains outwards. The whole incident was so bizarre that they and the beggar had no idea what to make of it.

As we walked on, my companions complained that I was taking food from the mouths of the starving. I, in turn, explained that I had taken the quarter in order to show them that there is always another view. I had chosen to see the beggar not as a being in need, but rather as a businessman who could affirm his abundance by giving. We took a table in a restaurant, and I placed the offending quarter on the center of the table just to bug 'em. Interestingly enough, when during dinner one of the molies had to make a phone call, he scooped up the beggar's quarter without a moment's hesitation and used it.

I think it's important to flip oneself and others into the contrary view, for it opens our minds to unusual possibilities. One day I invited a group of my best friends to a specialty restaurant that sold caviar, champagne, and very expensive Russian vodka. In those days, caviar cost around fifty dollars an ounce. Today it is more than double that. The idea of the meal was not to satisfy any nutritional need; rather, the object was to see how much money we could spend among six of us in just one hour. The maître d' was the timekeeper, and the guests and myself were the runners and riders, so to speak.

We began with Beluga caviar and Krug Krystal champagne and then progressed to other delicacies. The vodka was served ice cold in small glasses. At the end of each toast, we flung the glasses on the floor Russian style, shouting and cavorting. Everyone went bananas. For once there was no limit or consideration as to cost. It was very different. It was the most memorable meal of my life. We staggered out of the place an hour later drunk as lords, laughing our heads off. There was a sense of freedom and grandeur among us all. The tally came to around twelve hundred dollars at today's prices, or $20 a minute. Cheap, really, when you think we had fun and got a metaphysical lesson as well.

I think that it's a part of one's creative talent to make life different, to seek the contrary view. So it, in turn, contrasts the normal routine and makes that more interesting. In my last book, *Affirmations*, I deliberately left out a few words from the text. The first time this occurs, there is an asterisk that explains that the missing words in the book are dedicated to....Then I leave out who they are dedicated to. Further on in the book, the text suddenly starts going backwards for no explainable reason. It does so for just one paragraph. I get a steady stream of letters from readers protesting the typesetter's sloppy performance. The readers request a replacement copy. They don't get it.

Now, if you are reading a piece of text that suddenly goes backward, you can say, "The typesetter must have sat on his bifocals," or you can say, "I wonder what this pin-brained Limey author is trying to say." Could it be that in the missing words and backwards text there is a message?

There is the psychology of the non-being, and there is the etheric of the non-being. The etheric develops as discussed; the psychology you have to understand. It is no more than looking at the world from the reverse angle. Here's one more example. I was wandering the Souk in Marrakesh, when I became attracted to a leather bag hanging from one of the trader's stalls. I asked how much he wanted, and he replied, "10 diram." I shook my head and offered him 11 diram. He shook his head and said the best he could do was 9. I shook my head and insisted that I would pay no more than 12. He waved his arms about and told me about his wife and eight kids. Then he said it was daylight robbery, but he would, on this occasion, accept 7 diram and this was his very last offer. I "uhmed" and "ahed" and stroked my chin, and said that 15 was my final offer. He eventually agreed to sell me the bag for 5. At no time in the negotiation did he realize that I stood in the psychology of the non-being, going in the opposite direction. He agreed to take 5; I increased my offer to 17. His concentration was on the 5 diram he was about to get, my concentration was on the comedy of life. I wasn't about to contradict his reality. I paid him 5, thanked him, wishing him the strength of a hundred camels in the courtyard. I wandered on.

As one begins to look at all those areas in which one is not and begins to play the game of looking for the contrary view, one begins to consolidate oneself, affirming that the mind is the only power anyone will ever need. It can bring anything one sets one's heart on. Thus, there is no need to waste effort and energy thinking about things that are either untrue or worthless mental gyrations that can only bring anguish. Further, by constantly looking at the opposite in life, one can train the mind to see reality in all its ramifications. The mind can be trained to accept possibilities beyond its normal field of vision. One can expand and consolidate as a person.

In tick-tock, it is hard for people to accept the truth. They can't accept reality as they find it because they're uncomfortable and it threatens their self-image. So they bend the truth or avoid it altogether and play games to sustain a phony image. If you intend to consolidate and *quicken* your energy—as I am sure you do—you will find accepting the truth and living in it to be two of the most powerful concepts one can embrace.

Why is this so? Because once one can settle into what is real, into accepting the circumstances of life, then one can enter into a refreshing simplicity and live life through one's own energy, not through imagination. One affirms that one's alignment is not to the physical world with its egocentric play-acting but to the God-Force or infinity within, and that though one is a physical being, it is possible to accept that and live within that while centering at the same time on higher things.

You can only go past the world by going through it. There is honor in accepting your position, the humility of which grants you added attractiveness spiritually. Yet even humility can become phony. Looking at the various holy men with their loincloths and stark circumstances, one wonders if their humility comes from a genuine honesty or out of a self-flagellation that says, "I need to attract attention to my holiness, so if I accept these obscure practices, everyone will know that I am really holy, and they will respect me for that. It will make me special. Maybe I can start an ashram."

It is not the Warrior's way to make a show of his spirituality. In fact, he will deliberately hide it, making light of it. For anyone who has to talk about his holiness or to put it about is basically saying, "Look at me, I am favored in the eyes of God, I am chosen—better still, I am the voice of God, listen to what I have to say." They do so because in spite of their spirituality, they are firmly rooted in mechanical-man and need to feel special in order to create meaning in a life that they basically don't understand.

Look at the God-Force. It is everywhere. It is the most loving and spiritual asset we have, and yet it does not make a show of itself. In fact, it is hidden to most.

In the Warrior's way, one accepts what one is and pulls oneself back from all those places where one is not. If you want to reach your true power, you are forced, first, to accept things as they are; second, to live in the truth of what you are; and third, to control your mind and emotions so that they do not carry you away into a fantasy that would eventually become an affirmation of your lack.

If you say, "One day, someday, I will be rich," what you are affirming is that you will never make it, for you believe that you are not rich now. The Universal Law does not deal in future or past. It is. You have to be centered in the instant. For you to be rich, you have to feel rich right now. You have to see that what you have right now is wealth, a gift from the universe. You have to have patience, and you have to know and trust that you have all the goodness and power you will ever need, that opportunities will come to help you become more wealthy.

But more than anything else, you have to be in balance and in control wherever you find yourself. Otherwise, your imbalance stops more from coming. A person earning, say, $1,000 a month and who spends $1,500 a month, affirms his inability to accept circumstances and to balance his life. He is living in the reality of what he is not, saying, "I will design my life according to ego's needs, not according to what is truth—which in this case is $1,000 a month."

This character thinks that the way to solve his problems is to earn more money. In fact, earning more would be a disaster for him, but it is very likely that his imbalance will protect him from that anyway. If he were to suddenly double his income to $2,000, his spending pattern would go to $3,000, and then he would run a deficit of $1,000 a month, whereas before he was only running a deficit of $500. More than likely, the additional earning power would go to his head, and he might run a deficit even greater than $1,000 a month.

If suddenly he were to get $10,000 a month or even $100,000, his imbalance would be compounded, and he would collapse financially. It is not so much the imbalance that brings him down, it is the emotion of the imbalance that eventually permeates every aspect of his life. Every time a creditor presses him for a payment he does not have, it acts as an affirmation of his lie and creates a panic in him that affirms that he is out of control. Then, as he chases money to get out of trouble, his anguish and grinding need metaphysically push money away from him. Eventually, his income might even fall rather than increase, and he might find himself in even more trouble.

In order for people to give you money, they have to feel that there is balance and safety around the transaction. That is why it is rare for your bank to lend you money when you are out of control. They feel your panic and back away. In tick-tock, money is a symbol of security and survival. When mechanical-man parts with his cash, no matter how small the amount, there is a sense of loss. He has two thoughts: (1) I am becoming less important, I have less money, and (2) my ability to survive is lessened. So he spends money only if he feels safe and balanced, or if in purchasing something, he feels more important or more secure.

If a person who is out of control comes to mechanical-man and is desperate to get his cash, mechanical-man feels the desperation, the lack of stability, and it reminds him of all of his own fears. He backs off. Even if the deal is a good deal, mechanical-man will feel that perhaps he is being ripped off. He resents another trying to push the deal upon him. When one pushes for money, one sets up a wave of energy in front that is sustained by the emotion of one's need. That wave pushes up against reality and forces whatever opportunities there might be to move away—or at least to become harder to materialize.

I am sure you must have gone to buy a car having already decided what car you want, and as you walked into the showroom, a sleazy salesman, desperate for the commission, started to try to force you into the purchase, and you walked away to purchase the very same car at another showroom. Whenever we feel that someone is desperate in their need, we hesitate. Their desperation puts us off and makes us suspicious, angry, or both.

If one could interview a million people, one would find that they all have crushing needs. They all want something. They yearn for it. In their yearning, they usually never get what they want, and if, eventually, they do get it, then by the time it arrives, they don't want it anymore. This is because the emotional pleasure of the object or condition has been spent in their years of lack, so that when the object arrives, it is a bitter fruit, a symbol of their life-long yearning. In the wanting, they push. In their pushing and yearning, they project thoughts and feelings into their non-being; they weaken their power.

As a Warrior-Sage, you will adopt the contrary energy. You will pull. To do so, you'll design a lifestyle with as few needs as possible, which you rarely express to others. When the Warrior has a need, he uses his craft to get what he wants with minimum fuss, effort, or emotion. If you can get to a point of balance where your life is lived in truth, everything will be under control. That balance tells others that you are not in a rush. There is no panic. You walk slowly and you have time. It is an infinite approach. It says you are a part of all things, that you trust that all your needs are met, but it also says that you are different.

Then when you deal commercially with mechanical-man, he feels that security and balance within you. The poise you exude gives him pleasure. He feels more hopeful about his own survival, and as he transfers money to you, the sense of loss is diminished, for the transfer becomes an affirmation of his future. Further, he feels the infinity within you, and it seems to him that he is not losing anything in the deal, for he is transferring money to another part of himself.

As you develop the technique of pulling rather than pushing, there are several subtleties you should watch. It is common for people who embrace this idea to cast their fate to the wind, saying, "The Lord will provide." Yet the universe does not know what you need or when you need it. The timing and quality of events and the fulfillment of your needs is directed only by your emotions. If you cast your fate to the wind, what you affirm is that you don't control events, and so your lifestyle tends to reflect that. If you develop a trust in your power and affirm that your needs are met now so they are bound to be met in the future, then you go out into the marketplace of life and affirm that you are ready and able to allow the *inner you* to bring you to the right place at the right time so that you can take advantage of whatever opportunities are offered.

Tick-tock likes rhythm. That is why your bank likes you to commit to regular payments on certain days. Wouldn't it be nice if you could pay off your loans whenever you fancied, or not at all? But that is not the way. Knowing this, the Warrior tries as best he can to avoid financial commitments whenever possible, for commitments often lead to imbalance. People in the Western world usually have as much money as they will ever need, and that probably includes you. All your needs will be met. However, difficulty arises in the timing. If one looks at nature, one can see that it is abundant, but we also learn that it only delivers from time to time. You plant in the spring and nothing happens till August. The same often occurs with personal finances. You put out a lot of energy, and you have to wait for it to pay a dividend. We expect the abundance of the universe to pay out in little chunks at regular intervals, to fit the patterns we have obligated ourselves to. Often it doesn't.

Your best move is never to obligate yourself when you don't have to, and to try to win as much freedom within your obligation as possible. Otherwise, the negative emotion that occurs from that obligation is not worth whatever it is that you got. I am against personal loans from banks and credit companies, for in taking the loan, one affirms that one's abundance is not up to giving all that one desires, and so one borrows today from what is expected tomorrow. The loan becomes an affirmation of your lack of control, and sometimes merely satisfies an ego trip.

Commercial loans for businesses are different. In those circumstances, one usually borrows money to develop inventory or investment. You personally are not the end consumer. The money is usually in the business somewhere. It makes sense to borrow a controlled amount to enhance one's position in the market, but the big difference is that it is not being spent personally. The same with real estate mortgages. There, again, one is not a consumer. One borrows money to buy a house, the equity of which covers the loan. In the event of one's failure to pay, the house can be sold, and one can settle the obligation. The thing to watch here is that one doesn't commit to payments greater than one can comfortably sustain.

Finances are not the only place where one's consciousness lives a fake reality. Our relationships often contain the same unreal qualities, because we are too weak to tell others what we really feel or think about the relationship. This is not the place to deal with what is a complex subject. But you know if your relationships are real or if they are not. And you know how to fix them if need be. We learn about ourselves through relationships because they reflect what we are back to us. If you are surrounded by nonsense, that means you have allowed nonsense to establish itself in your life. Simple, really. If your relationships are loving and empowering, that means that you are, also.

The name of the game is to review all your relationships from time to time to assess what it is you contribute and what it is you receive in return (a spot check of the heart chakra). Relationships change so quickly that it should be a part of your modus to institute quality control into every aspect of your life. If you are not getting what you want or if you are putting in all the effort and the others are contributing little, it will become obvious. Then you must decide if that is acceptable to you or not. If not, you will diplomatically indicate what your needs are and suggest that they fulfill them. In turn, you find out what they want. If both of you want something different and things can't be resolved, do not be afraid to release them or to walk away yourself.

The Warrior relies on no one, and no one is indispensable. He won't allow that situation to develop. If a person has that kind of hold on you, then you must ask yourself how you let that develop and what you can do about it. So often we blame those around us for making us miserable. Yet we omit noticing our responsibility in the matter. How many business people have you heard complain that their staff is useless, that they are surrounded by idiots who are wrecking the business? If that is your case, why have you not pulled Warriors to your cause? Why have you deliberately chosen Bozos and flakes to support your efforts? If you have, then who are you going to blame? The world is full of useless people. In fact, it is accurate to say that most of the world is mediocre, and the rest of the world is flapping like crazy hoping to make mediocre.

It is the Warrior's way to be selective. This is not a judgment on those he omits, just selection. It is better that you have two or three powerful Warrior-Sage types around you than a host of wimps. In the *Quickening,* you are looking to use your time and efforts economically. The cast of characters you select for your life is vital. They affirm your strength, or they assist in confirming your weakness. Why waste effort trying to get someone who's weak and distracted to pull their weight? It's simpler to toss them out and hire a character who will take responsibility and deliver.

Isn't it true that very few people are prepared to do a decent job? They provide just the bare minimum, and even that is performed with reluctance. Then they charge as much as they feel they can get away with, and their mind is rarely on the job. They skip across the surface of life, expecting the world to support them and get very upset when it does not. In contrast, the Warrior-Sage commits to his or her life and lives it. His attention is on the quality of his actions. He knows that those around him are a reflection of himself, so he chooses wisely. In taking responsibility, he follows through. He does whatever he finds in front of him, and he guarantees you that you will get all you ever expect and more. If need be, he puts in a few extra hours at his own expense in order to follow through. The world constantly ducks out of responsibility, blaming others, or it seeks to avoid taking responsibility or having to deliver on its commitments.

I have always disliked contracts and legal agreements. But I found that in tick-tock they are a necessity. One has to spell out what it is that one expects of other people; otherwise they rarely follow through on their word. There is little honor nowadays, and honesty is not highly regarded either. Perhaps this is because our leaders are seen to be dishonest, so we raise our children with inferior role models. Perhaps the world is too crowded and too frantic for honor. Perhaps because in our day-to-day dealings with institutions we are so often treated as potentially dishonest, we take on that hue. We see everyone in that, light, and, projecting that opinion on others, we collectively get what we project— a world of shady people.

In dealing with corporations and suppliers, it is always mind-boggling to me how it is that we will get a quote on a job, and then when the bills comes in, the price is often well in excess of the agreement. They bid low to get the job, and then stiff us on the final bill. Or included on the bill are several additional, spurious charges that they hope won't be noticed or argued over. Recently, we got a bill for about $700 from a company in Florida for photocopying supplies. As we were about to pay it, we realized we did not have a packing slip or delivery note for the goods. On searching we could not find the goods either. So we wrote to the company for proof of delivery, and that was the last we ever heard from them. It seems they just tossed us out a bill, hoping that we would pay it without checking to see whether or not we had received the goods.

Because the Warrior sees his life as a symbol of what he is, he ensures that his every act is imbued with truth, honesty, and honor. These he feels because of his acceptance of the enormity of life. It is as though his cause, placed as it is in his heart, cannot be detached from the physical manifestations of itself. As the Warrior is not concerned with survival, he has no need of skimping over or dealing in a shabby way with people. His honor becomes an affirmation of what he is. He pulls to himself people who are honorable, or at least the most honest available. Further, because he is not concerned with status, he can turn his hand to any task, seeing it as a chance to refine what he is. Thus, placing himself into everything he does and not judging his worth by his position, he allows himself to get the most out of life, perfecting what he is by concentrating on what he is doing.

When on rare occasions he fails, he forgives himself and vows to do better the next time. That way his successes ride with him while his mishaps become a part of his total learning and are then released. He seeks in each day the honor of just being a part of that day, and he can see value in all of his actions no matter how mundane.

It is interesting that societies based on honor always prosper, and those that are not so based eventually fail. A prime example of this is Japan. The Japanese dedication and the honor they hold for their cause and for each other have made their society second to none in the world. Island nations have an advantage over others because they naturally band together and hold to a common ideal. Being half Sicilian and half British, I have been able to study the history and to watch firsthand how island societies develop.

When you look at the British, it's hard to imagine how they succeeded in conquering a third of the world. The country is small and has very few resources. Napoleon called them "a nation of shopkeepers," and that's what they are. But how did they develop an empire? It baffled me until I realized that Britain had all the earmarks of an occult society. It was developed around ritual, honor, and chivalry. It was the first modern nation to form a parliament and develop individual rights. In addition, the people are dedicated to the monarchy and to the nation, and, finally, the British are naturally secretive. Most of the modern secret service borrowed heavily from the British M15. It is hard to get a Brit to open up his heart and discuss how he feels. Some would say the British are covert, and that, perhaps, is true. But that same closed or stiff-upper-lip aspect helped the nation build a powerful energy. The British are used to "making do." They plow out regardless of the suffering or danger. Comfort is not an overriding issue. The colonialists who conquered the world were few in number, but they were dedicated and disciplined, and they got the job done.

Things have changed since the war, and much of the old honor and high ideals have been replaced in the hearts of the common people by the government's philosophy of equal poverty for all. But there still remains in those Isles the understanding that a man is only as good as his word, and that personal gain should not overshadow "doing the right thing." It seems that the epitome of the Warrior mentality is to get things done, no matter what, while staying within the bounds of honor. So many in the world want everything perfect before they can make their moves. As the Warrior, one can relish adversity and plow on, regardless. All the nonsense that says that things have to be fair, cozy, and convenient is just a Charter of Wimpdom. One faces life as it comes. If you find yourself at a disadvantage, outnumbered, with people actively pushing against you, realize that the circumstances you face allow you to prove to yourself that you have the strength, tenacity, and cunning of a hundred people in tick-tock.

13

EXERCISES IN TURBO-THOUGHT

Most of our thoughts, being ruminations, border on day-dreams and have little psychic tension or strength. In contrast, turbo-thoughts have etheric power and intensity and are pointed. They impact one's destiny with vigor.

For your consciousness to have that kind of strength, you first have had to clear the decks. This means that by now you will have consolidated your life, and you will be comfortable concentrating on just that. Thus, when creating thoughts that you want to have a special effect on your life, you are at least coming from a centered, uncompromised position, clear in your intention and forceful in your desire.

I can best explain turbo-thought by recounting how it was that I was first exposed to the idea. A teacher of mine in Europe taught me to project thoughts to others, forcing them to react. The first exercise he gave me was to go to the lobby of a large hotel, and, using only a concentrated projection of my mind, induce people with their backs toward me to turn around. He recommended concentrating on the back of the neck of those targeted, and to create the feeling that I was, in fact, standing right up close to that person, breathing down his or her neck. Once this feeling was established, I was to imagine licking the back of the person's neck. Sounds awful, but it isn't, really.

I tried it. Amazingly enough, I found that I could get almost all of them to turn—some more readily than others. It was only when the individual was engaged in some activity that dominated his concentration, that he failed to notice my etheric maneuvers. Try it for yourself; you'll be amazed. Lest you think it an infringement, suffice it to say that I don't feel that having people turn around is an act that greatly affects them. I feel fine about it.

Another exercise is to find a park bench that is beside a footpath and to sit there absolutely still, moving not a muscle, not a hair, blinking as little as possible. The idea is to establish an area of energy around you that is outside normal reality—an etheric free zone. Nothing animate is ever completely still. Once that motionless calm is around you, imagine yourself holding a stick across the path at the height of a few inches. Then, keeping your concentration solely on the stick at all times and reinforcing that image with your mind, watch the passersby trip on the nonexistent stick! If you find this hard at first, grant yourself an added boost: As they approach, imagine your open hand giving them a hefty shove in the back. That'll do it.

They won't fall on their nose. At best they will stutter-step, but that is enough, and you won't necessarily get them all, but you will get some. When you do, you will know that you can easily create turbo-thought, and that that thought can be used in many fascinating ways.

Here's one more exercise you can try. Energize a sewing needle by rubbing it on a magnet. Place the needle horizontally in a dish of water. Relax yourself into a meditative state. Then using just your mind, force the needle to move in the water. To ensure that your breath does not affect the needle, place your hand in front of your nose and mouth. You'll get a lot of pleasure in seeing the needle move.

The reasons for these exercises is party fun. But also they help you realize that the power vested by God in your mind is immense. Whenever you create thought that comes out of psychic intensity, you will find that your visualization or image will materialize quickly in front of you. It is in part like skipping across reality, in part intention, and in part the velocity of the thought.

Many create turbo-thought naturally, but they are not disciplined in their projections, so the results are a bit hit or miss. I am sure that you have experienced times of incredible clarity where for a few hours you really felt that you had managed to get out of your own way, that you were invincible.

In the '88 Super Bowl between the Denver Broncos and the Washington Redskins, the Broncos had a commanding ten-point lead by the end of the first quarter. There then followed one of the most remarkable 15 minutes in football history. The Redskins went into turbo-thought, and their quarterback, Doug Williams, the first black quarterback ever to play in the Super Bowl, threw one incredible touchdown after another. By the half, the Redskins had breezed past the Broncos, leading 35 to 10. Doing so, they set several Super Bowl records. It was all over. The Redskins had hit turbo-thought and blew Denver out of the water. How did they do it? I am sure they don't know. They just decided to win. The psychic intensity was there, and everything dropped naturally into place.

When one breaks out of the sluggishness of normal thought, the excitement of power throws such a weight behind one's consciousness that one can agree with the *inner self* on anything. It amazes me how some people with AIDS suddenly and mysteriously agree to heal themselves. They are only a small percentage, but their inner etheric decides to live, and so the virus disappears. It's marvelous—one of many superhuman feats available to us in turbo-thought.

Whenever a thought is laced with the intensity of the etheric, it is automatically several hundred times stronger than normal thoughts. In the example of an illness or a ball game, the turbo-thought effect is created by desires and an overriding confidence in one's power. But this happens only rarely. To create turbo-thought whenever you need it, you use the simple technique of adjusting your mind, first, to accept a vastly enhanced possibility (that is, you agree to believe it) and, second, to use the full force of your concentration and Life Force laced into the thought.

This involves enthusiasm and caring. You must genuinely want the condition you have set your mind on. You must know it to be a fact. You must care about it. Imagine it as a small child that you love, that you have agreed to look after. Then you must feel as though the fact is already granted and real. Then in a meditative state, place your concentration at the root chakra, at the base of the spine in the genital region. Know that there is your etheric storehouse, and slowly pull from that base, with your mind, a quantum of energy. You can visualize it as a ball of light. See that energy moving slowly up an imaginary line through the center of your body, like an elevator. You will have decided, prior to this, which of three chakras—heart, throat, or third eye—is your strongest. (You can't use the crown chakra for turbo-thought.) If you don't know which is your strongest chakra, intuitively guess. Then, as you move the Life Force up your body, stop it once it reaches the chosen chakra, and hover it there for a moment.

Allow the energy of the chakra and the energy that you have raised from the root to mix. By now, that image of light will be held slightly outside your body at a distance of about an inch.

Place inside that pellet of energy your visualized intention. Allow the etheric energy that you have collected from the root to infuse your image so that the visualization becomes a hologram, so that within every atom of the etheric energy there is contained a complete image of the whole. Feel that image excited and intensified by the Life Force. Say, for example, that you want to live and work in Paris as a successful artist. To be effective, you would have to know what Paris felt like, its ambience. You also would have to be able to see yourself there, working in that way. It has to be real, an image you can believe. Not just one you hope for. You have to feel excited by the possibility; there should be no apprehension or fear. Then, when you have held that image inside the pellet of energy and you have hovered it there for a brief moment to stabilize it, you are ready to fire the turbo-thought. This is accomplished in two ways depending on whether or not your thought is to be directed away from you, at someone else, or if it is to stay with you to create a new condition.

Let us first take the example of creating new circumstances. This type of turbo-thought does not leave you. In firing it, you explode it all around you, top to bottom, left to right, behind and in front, so that the energized hologram of your visualization enters every molecule of what you are. In this way, every minute part of your mind-body-spirit now contains the image of your new circumstances. Your destiny pattern, which lays all around you in your etheric, now contains the new possibility as fact.

To explode the thought, expel from your mouth a short burst of air that you originate from the lower diaphragm. It is like a forceful sigh. As you express it, your stomach muscles will contract. The sigh will be akin to a sniff, except that you are exhaling rather than inhaling. Simultaneously, see the pellet with your image in it, explode, blasting and radiating through your entire being. Once the explosion is completed, release the idea, and do not think about it for at least 72 hours. To make turbo-thought work for you, you have to position yourself emotionally away from the idea once it is fired. There can be no harassing the thought with negative yearning, or you'll destroy its effect. After three days, if you wish, you can give the idea another burst, and so on. Then release it again.

As to the firing of a turbo-thought at another person, let us create a scenario as an example so that the concept is simpler to understand. Say you wanted to influence a person to give you a certain job that was your heart's desire. As you enter the interview, you could turbo-thought your way into the position. Now some might say this was an infringement, and in certain circumstances, I would agree with them. If you are genuinely living the Warrior-Sage, honor is a part of your life. You are not going to do anything untoward. Your getting the job will greatly benefit that organization as you will bring to it a special power. The benefit to them will be greater than it will be to you.

If you rested in tick-tock, a turbo-thought to the interviewer would certainly be manipulative and would border on black magic. But if you are coming out of Warrior-Sage, the projection of your thought contains the goodness of the God-Force and that is intrinsically balanced. Therefore, things will unfold to everyone's highest good. In this example of turbo-thought, you are going to attempt to get inside the mind of the interviewer. The object of the exercise is not to infringe on him in any way. Rather, you are trying to infuse the situation with Life force and excitement. You want to raise his energy so that he is inspired by your presence.

Let me give you the method, then I will leave it up to you to come from a place of honor and strength and to add to the liberation of the world rather than to its manipulation. First, you would set the groundwork by granting yourself every advantage possible. You would select a position in front of the interviewer, with your chair slightly at an angle to him, not directly opposite.

This is more relaxing for him than a head-on position. As he or she spoke, you would concentrate solely on their forehead at the space between their eyes. During the interview, keep your body motionless: It is your power pose. The stillness would create in the mind of the interviewer, consciously or unconsciously, the feeling that he is dealing with a person of unusual qualities. Any motion you might have to make should be slow and deliberate. When asked a question, you should pause for at least a second or two before answering. The pause allows you to dominate the interview even though it will seem on the surface that you do not. Before delivering your response, you should lean back ever so slightly in your chair; the pause and lean pull the interviewer into your energy field. You would strategically drop your voice whenever you wanted to make an important point. The soft voice is another pulling technique. It forces the interviewer to lean toward you to hear your answer. Your responses should be informative and to the point. Be sure that you repeat at least three times that you are happy to take responsibility, you like responsibility, and you can't live without it. Also, be sure that you let him know that you are a supporter; you'll back his cause. You are not a terrorist who will organize the workers in a mass walkout.

In discussing the job or life, you would voice no criticism or judgment or negativity of any kind. If the interviewer says, "Life's a bitch," do not disagree with him—just don't answer. When responding to his questions, your replies should include some rhetorical questions to the interviewer, especially questions that let him talk about himself. This will open him up. "How long have you worked here, sir?" "Three years," he replies. You say, "I see, so you climbed to position of such responsibility in just three years. It seems like an exciting company to work for."

Now for the turbo-thought. First, decide if the interviewer is left-handed or right-handed. If need be, ask him. If he wants to know why you have asked, tell him you are interested in handwriting or something like that. If asking is awkward, then invent a reason for him to write something down for you. Watch which hand he uses. You'll need this information.

As he talks, pull a quantum of Life Force up from your root chakra and hover it at your power point. See yourself inside that ball of energy. If you like, you can imagine yourself as a little person inside that bubble. Have the little person say your name; that allows you to strengthen the feeling that the image there is actually you. Imagine the little-you inside the bubble as an astronaut poised, ready to be launched into the cosmos.

You are going to fire that turbo-thought into the interviewer's mind. Thus, you visualize a line of light entering the interviewer via his root chakra, running up his spine into his right brain. Fire your thought-form along the line of light, expelling a short breath as you do so. Have the thought-form explode in his brain, like a shower of God-Force.

There are several points to make here. Going through the root chakra of the interviewer should not have any sexual connotation whatsoever. If it does, you lower the quality of your mental projection. The root chakra is just the open doorway that you use, nothing more. If the interviewer is left-handed, then fire the thought-form into his left brain. That is important. You are looking to influence the spatial, creative, feeling side of his brain, not his intellect. You want him to feel excited about life, not to think it's a nice day. The feeling is stronger.

Right-handed people usually have their intellectual logical self, situated mostly in the left brain. So to a right-handed person, your turbo-thought goes to his opposite side, his right brain, where his feelings rest, away from his logic, to his infinite, inner self. People who write with their left hand are reversed. They have logic in their right brain and feelings in the left brain, so you have to watch that.

Once the thought is fired, back off. If you have been successful, you will notice him blink or react to your projection. If nothing happens, wait a moment and try again. If you know the hit has been made, allow the infusion of your energy to take hold. Don't overdo it. Too much energy, and the interviewer will become restless and distracted.

The point of this technique is to project into the person etheric Life Force that has been infused by you. It won't necessarily get you the job, but it will create in the mind of the interviewer a positive feeling toward you. He will feel more secure. That is a great help to you. This kind of turbo-thought is much like expressing love to another, except it is powerful and pointed and less airy-fairy than just *thinking* love.

The same turbo-thought technique can be used at a distance when the target person is at a different location from you. In these circumstances, you have to have a very strong idea as to the feeling of the person's character. If possible, you should also be able to visualize that person accurately. At a distance, your concentration has to be more acute, but the firing is the same as it would be if he or she were seated in front of you. If you don't know whether the person is predominantly right-brained or left, just ask your intuition and go with the answer.

One caution here. When firing a thought at another, it should always be pure Life Force. If it should contain a desire that you are trying to infuse into the mind of another, then it becomes an infringement. Generally, the individual will have no way of stopping you. He will feel that whatever thought you have offered is, in fact, his, and he may act contrary to his normal disposition.

I know a female metaphysician of dubious repute who uses sexually active etheric to get what she wants from men. She told me she got a loan from her bank manager by going into the etheric and masturbating him while he considered her loan.

It is not for me to judge or comment. But once you get into this kind of practice, the temptation can carry you away from goodness into devilry. I can't see a Warrior-Sage ever needing something so badly that he would stoop to borderline practices to get it. The morality of turbo-thought is that you manipulate yourself into a heightened reality rather than manipulate others. In the gamut of possibilities, you have to be the judge as to what is right or wrong.

Here is another example to ponder: I know of people who use turbo-thought while playing sports. They get inside the mind of the opposition, confusing them and putting them off their game. They are very successful at it. In this instance, I don't see that as too much of an infringement, for in the competition of a game, each pits his gamesmanship and skill against the other. The fact that the right-winger is a Warrior-Sage is a part of the hazards of a competitive world.

In closing, let us discuss good and evil. The God-Force does not judge, so from its perspective there is no good or evil. Morality is just an opinion affected by one's stance in reality. However, within the deeds of man we can see that certain acts are infringing and restrictive, while others are liberating and loving. We can choose whatever direction we wish, and we live with the consequence of our selection.

In tick-tock, which is dominated so much by fear, sin, and evil, negativity is repressed in the psyche for fear that those aspects might run amok and destroy the individual. However, there is only the one energy in the universe. Good and evil are only different aspects of that one energy.

As your power grows, your ability to create goodness expands. Yet within that heightened perspective, you have to carry the seeds of your own destruction. This means that you cannot develop power in one direction without simultaneously opening yourself up to the other. The higher you climb, the greater the possibility of your fall.

So the Warrior-Sage does not shun the negative. He accepts

its reality and stays disciplined and mindful at all times to ensure that his acts stem from the highest good. When your perspective is limited, your ability to infringe is also limited. As you grow, your possibility for evil grows with you. To run away from that is not realistic. You have to accept that and stay within what you know to be honest, loving, and good.

14

OCCULT BROTHERHOODS AND THE CUNNING OF THE MONGOLS

IT SEEMS a shame, when reading of the occult brotherhoods and orders of knights of yesteryear, to think that nowadays none such honorable brotherhoods exist. Imagine the excitement of being admitted to, say, the order of the Teutonic Knights, to ride in the company of other knights, and to seek one's fortune in the Holy Land or attack the infidel in some holy cause.

Modern life demands that our quests be more mundane. Our heroic deeds are limited to making the car payments on time. Yet, is there a place for the chivalry of old? Could we perhaps devise a plan whereby elements of the "unexpected" once again dominate our lives? It is nice to think that we could.

In the modern cult of the Warrior-Sage, we see "quest" expressed as an individual journey. Gone are the brotherhoods of monks and knights; nowadays we strive for spiritual understanding on our own. Perhaps that is how it is supposed to be. But one can't help wondering if perhaps the old glories could not be re-created.

Certainly, if a group of powerful individuals gather, dedicating themselves to a cause, they can usually bring that cause to fruition. They have to be silent and disciplined, otherwise the group has no power. That has been the problem with many consciousness-raising groups that formed over the years. They often failed. The groups gathered to help each other grow, and as they achieved that growth, the power of the individuals became so intense that they began to infringe, each upon the other, and eventually the group either became suffocating or it disintegrated.

There are many symbols of the Warrior-Sage that we can draw on for inspiration. Besides the Chinese cults of Warrior-Monks such as Shao-lin and their Buddhist Japanese equivalent, we can look to societies such as the Knights Templar—an occult brotherhood of Christian Gnostics who defended Christendom as well as selling their military service in return for lands and wealth.

But for me, the Mongols were the quintessence of the Warrior, and I have based a whole teaching, called the Warrior's Wisdom, around Mongolian philosophy. People may ask how I am able to find spiritual worth in the ideals of a barbaric society such as the Mongols. Yet if one understands their time in history, it is apparent that the Mongols were far from barbaric. It is true that they were a fierce and violent people, but they had within their philosophy a softness and a special mysticism that exhibited, in my view, all the qualities of the Warrior-Sage. The Mongols were written up as barbarians by the European historians because for the most part the historians were on the receiving end of the Mongol thrust, so they were unlikely to say anything good about the Tartars, as they were called. History was bent toward the European view.

One example of this is the story of good King Wenceslas. It was written that this heroic king went out and beat the Mongols and thus saved his people. In fact when the Mongols advanced into Bohemia, Wenceslas took all of his knights and the members of his court and retreated 70 miles south, leaving the rest of his subjects to their fate. A scouting party of Mongol horsemen was dispatched to look for him. This party, which consisted of 300 warriors, was attacked by Wenceslas' knights and beaten off. Thus, the legend grew that Wenceslas had defeated the Tartars and saved Christendom. In fact, he did no such thing. Eventually the Mongols, realizing he was no threat, ignored his presence to the south and rode around him. Wenceslas never engaged the Mongols in battle.

In looking at the overall picture, one has to understand that the 13th century was not a time for human rights; it was a time when man learned to step out of his boundaries, both geographic and mental. The Renaissance was around the next corner. In Christian Europe, one could be hung for stealing a loaf of bread. In China, one could lose one's head for not bowing to a noble. Yet in Mongolian law, the Yasa, there were only two crimes punishable by death: adultery and cattle or horse rustling. Conditions in Europe for the common people were terrible. They were for the most part serfs of the landed gentry, and, as such, lived as slaves. In Mongolia, once the tribes were united by Genghis Khan, each man was free. There was order, law, and a way of doing things. The only slaves, as such, came from outside the Mongolian tribes.

What we learn from the Mongols, we can use today. They had cunning and discipline, and they were organized. In fact, the Mongolian word for an encampment, *orda*, gave birth to our word *order*. We can see in the way they developed their strategies that their generals were brilliant. Indeed, the Mongolian battle plans have been used throughout history, and as recently as the Second World War, by both Patton and Rommel in the North African campaign.

But more than anything else, we see in the Mongol warrior his fluidity and his ability to transcend conditions and stay focused on the target. The Mongol army was sustained on horse-back. So the horse was revered, and battle horses were never slaughtered for food—in fact, they were often buried with their warrior owners. It is an amazing fact that when the Mongols departed on their second European campaign, they took with them a million horses. Both Mongol rider and horse were imper-vious to hardship. The warrior slept in the saddle, and if he found himself on a long journey without water, he would slit a vein in the horse's neck, drink its blood, and then bandage the animal and ride on. The army could ride in the severest of conditions, and they traveled faster than any other army of their time. Usually, armies traveled at the rate of 20 miles a day, if they were lucky. The Mongols could move 60,000 men up to 100 miles a day when pushed. Mobility was the key to their success. In addition, the simplicity of their lifestyle and the uncluttered way they designed their fighting units gave them a tremendous advantage over the heavily armored cavalry of their opponents.

The Mongol army was divided up into decimal units of 10,000 men (tumens) and then units of 1,000 men (jurgans) and eventually down to units of 10 men (arbans). Like the Roman army, the troops drilled constantly so that every man knew his position in the line. The commanders used whistling arrows, drums, and a rudimentary system of flag signals similar to sema-phore to communicate with their troops. Thus, they were able to move very large blocks of horsemen instantaneously.

The Empire was laced by a pony express system that was developed by Genghis Khan so that he could be in constant touch with every corner of it. Staging posts were set every few miles, and riders constantly tracked back and forth. They wore belts made with bells. As they approached a staging post, the guardians of the post would hear bells and make ready a fresh horse.

The life of Temujin (Genghis Khan) has many metaphysical lessons for us to learn. He started in adverse conditions with a tribe of 17, which included his mother. He let nothing stop him from his quest, which he believed was God given. He was a great warrior, but also a diplomat. Once he had conquered or aligned the Mongolians, which he completed in 1212, he set out to develop treaties with his neighbors. He knew the benefit of diplomacy, and many castles and lands were won through treaty without a fight.

The Mongolian philosophy was greatly influenced by the Taoists in China, which they captured in 1215. The philosophy, like Taoism, reveals a deep respect for nature. They venerated the sky, the moon, and the stars. Included in their practices was a dawn ritual to the sun. Like the Taoists they had the deepest respect for water. Rivers were considered sacred, and washing or urinating in the waters was forbidden. Of the four elements, fire was considered the most sacred.

The Mongols believed in an infinite Universal Presence, and their shamans held some of the most influential positions in their hierarchy. It was from these Mongolian shamans that Magic, as we know it today, was developed. They held the key to the spiritual thrust of the Mongol intent, as did the generals' rule over the policies and directions of the armies. The shaman acted partly as a healer and partly as an advisor. They were spiritualists, and they communicated with the gods in the spirit world in trance ecstasies, in which the shaman would visit the etheric world of heaven (Shamballa) or the underworld and bring back information. As a part of their culture, they believed in life after death, and they had complex rituals to the dead.

The Mongol women traveled with their men on the various campaigns. They acted as supporters and healers, and on some occasions they fought beside the men. After the defeat of the Hungarian army at Mohi (A.D. 1241) east of modern-day Budapest, fearful tales went about as to the strength of the Mongols, but what impressed the writers most was the fierceness of the women who had also fought in battle.

What we learn from the Mongols is craftiness, simplicity, mobility, and the ability to accept circumstances. They were an inspiration, for they were unstoppable. If you set your mind to the same intensity—toward a goal or quest—that Mongolian spirit will serve you well. You are bound to achieve your goal for you, too, become unstoppable. Each time you fall, you rise again. If you fall 10 times, you rise 11. If you fall 100 times, you rise up for the 101st time. You agree with yourself that you will never quit. There are no conditions that can stop you—not sickness, circumstances, or fortune. All will be plowed under by the force of your intent.

It seems that today we have no great causes worthy of our attention, and the popular world causes seem to me ineffectual and unattractive. Perhaps the function of the Warrior-Sage today is only unto himself. Or perhaps the rebirth of the Warrior individual is the way that our world will eventually be saved from itself. Who knows?

It is possible that the time of the Warrior-Sage has not yet come. Perhaps we will not live to see it. But our children will inherit that strength, and, coming as they do out of less inhibition than their parents, they will rise up to form a new spirituality. From that they will demand a new world beyond manipulation, beyond the hackneyed "twaddle" that binds us today.

The New Age movement is a protest against that institutional "twaddle" that has been handed down through generations. We seek within our own quest some higher ideal; a philosophy that will take us from the restriction of a tick-tock rhythm into a higher, freer, more loving, more purposeful life. Yet when we look at the New Age, we can laugh at ourselves, for within the movement are the makings of a comic "twaddle" second-to-none. As we sought to discover ourselves, we left no stone unturned in our effort to embrace silliness. We dug up our past lives, shook hands with our guides, rubbed our little crystals, and invented all manner of bizarre practices in our effort to understand ourselves. In the end, was the philosophy we acquired a powerful affirmation of our individuality, or did we discard some old hackneyed religion for a new set of restrictive practices that were equally moronic?

Often, what the New Age created were warriors of the "soggy Kleenex" variety—people just as weak as those left behind. Isn't it true, if you were looking for a group of people to hash up a project, all you had to do was form a New Age committee and that would fix it once and for all.

Yet we meant well. We wanted the world to see a new way. We wanted a world of brotherhood, with tolerance and opportunity for all. And we insisted on the freedom of developing an individualized personal relationship with the Force. Certainly our hearts were in the right place, even though our heads were in the clouds.

Then the movement took on a *Quickening*—it grew up. We found we had to come off the mountaintop and back into the marketplace in order to exercise our power. Suddenly, things began to work. We created strong individuals: self-assured, balanced, silent, secretive, perhaps. We created the Warrior-Sage, able to operate effectively inside society—not avoiding it or living apart from it.

Gone was the whiny, wimpy "miso-stain-on-the-Indian-skirt" philosophy. In its place was the power of the spiritual warrior, an individual beyond tick-tock, beyond the manipulations of man, unafraid to express himself or to wield his power if he had to.

In the cult of the Warrior-Sage, we see a new form of spirituality based on naturalness, truth, and an unpretentious lifestyle. We no longer have to plead with God by doing "holy-moly" things, hoping that the Force will somehow favor our ineptitude. Now we demand the perception and power we know is our birthright, and we settle in the spirituality of being ourselves, of accepting self. We are happy to be real and to live life in truth. We are no longer trying to accommodate everyone to win their affection. That's over. No more excuses, no more explaining ourselves. "I am what I am. If that pleases you, great. If it doesn't, eat it!"

The Warrior knows he is not perfect, but he is content with what he is and where he finds himself. Tick-tock is dominated by the ego, the primary motivation or which is survival. People want to know that life will be cozy, safe, and guaranteed. The Warrior, detached as he is from his death, is not looking to survive. He concentrates instead on living, experiencing each moment to the fullest, knowing it may be his last. He accepts circumstances as they come even if they are uncomfortable, dangerous, and uncertain. He realizes that many of the mysteries of life will always remain hidden, so he settles comfortably into "not knowing" and turns his attention from pondering the future into concentrating on the present and whatever he finds in front of him.

By concentrating on your own life, you become powerful. You can't help the world with fine ideals. First, you have to become strong. Cut out all distractions. Drop off the "wimpos" at the bus stop and dedicate yourself to your own quest, nothing else. Realize that dedication is the Warrior's prayer unto himself. To try to fix the world is an infringement on it. The Warrior knows that his power comes from leaving things alone, for mechanical-man will change only when he is good and ready. All you can offer the world is your strength, your honor, and the quality of your quest exemplified by your life.

The New Age does not need 100 million converts in order to change the world. It only needs a few people who are good warriors and true. One man took Buddhism from India to China.

In the next decade, you will see the mechanical world of tick-tock unravel as never before. If you give your power away to the institutions, circumstances will eat your lunch. If you step inside the Warrior-Sage philosophy, you are left with just yourself, but at least you are left with a person you can trust.

P.S. THANK YOU. This book, *The Quickening*, concludes my quintet of books on metaphysical self-empowerment. (The other titles are *Miracles, The Trick to Money Is Having Some, The Force*, and *Affirmations*.) I would like to thank each and every one of you who have purchased and read my books for your support, without which none of this would have been possible. Good strength on your quest, and may the sweet scent of true freedom ride as your constant companion.

Sincerely,
Stuart Wilde
Taos, New Mexico

TREE EXERCISE

Go out into a wooded area at dusk. Pick a large, robust tree, preferably one that has abundant foliage. Put yourself into a relaxed state and place your concentration at the top of the tree at the twelve o'clock position.

Next, move your eye to the right, staring for a moment, at the sky beside the tree where one o'clock would be. Then without moving your eyes from that position, take your concentration back to the top of the tree.

You will see the etheric Life Force of the tree expressing itself dynamically to a distance of up to three or five feet around the tree. It will look like a gray-blue wispy trails of vibrant energy. Whereas the tree may seem static, by looking at its inner regality you will notice that it is in fact lively and constantly changing. You may also come to the perception that the tree has an identity; it is part of all living things as you are. You and the tree are one.

ABOUT THE AUTHOR

Author and lecturer Stuart Wilde is one of the real characters of the self-help, human potential movement. His style is humorous, controversial, poignant, and transformational. He has written 13 books, including those that make up the very successful Taos Quintet, which are considered classics in their genre. They are: *Affirmations*, *The Force*, *Miracles*, *The Quickening*, and *The Trick to Money Is Having Some*. Stuart's books have been translated into 12 languages.

**STUART WILDE International Tour
and Seminar Information:**

For information on Stuart Wilde's latest tour and
seminar dates in the USA and Canada, contact:

White Dove International
P.O. Box 1000, Taos, NM 87571
(505) 758-0500 phone
(505) 758-2265 fax

Stuart's Website:
www.stuartwilde.com

We hope you enjoyed this Hay House book.
If you would like to receive a free catalog featuring additional
Hay House books and products, or if you would like information about
the Hay Foundation, please contact:

Hay House, Inc.
P.O. Box 5100
Carlsbad, CA 92018-5100

(760) 431-7695 or (800) 654-5126
(760) 431-6948 (fax) or (800) 650-5115 (fax)
www.hayhouse.com

Published and distributed in Australia by:
Hay House Australia Pty Ltd, P.O. Box 515, Brighton-Le-Sands, NSW
2216 • *phone:* 1800 023 516 • *e-mail:* info@hayhouse.com.au

Distributed in the United Kingdom by:
Airlift, 8 The Arena, Mollison Ave., Enfield, Middlesex,
United Kingdom EN3 7NL

Distributed in Canada by:
Raincoast, 9050 Shaughnessy St., Vancouver, B.C., Canada V6P 6E5